# WRITING THE SACRED

A PSALM-INSPIRED PATH

to appreciating

and writing

SACRED POETRY

RAY McGINNIS

# Writing THE Sacred

A PSALM-INSPIRED PATH
to appreciating
and writing
SACRED POETRY

Northstone

EDITORS: MICHAEL SCHWARTZENTRUBER, HEATHER PICOTTE
COVER AND INTERIOR DESIGN: MARGARET KYLE
PROOFREADING: DIANNE GREENSLADE
COVER ARTWORK: WWW.PHOTOS.COM –
ADAPTED BY MARGARET KYLE

Northstone is an imprint of Wood Lake Publishing, Inc. Wood Lake Publishing acknowledges the financial support of the Government of Canada, through the Book Publishing Industry Development Program (BPIDP) for its publishing activities. Wood Lake Publishing also acknowledges the financial support of the Province of British Columbia through the Book Publishing Tax Credit.

At Wood Lake Publishing, we practise what we publish, being guided by a concern for fairness, justice, and equal opportunity in all of our relationships with employees and customers. Wood Lake Publishing is an employee-owned company, committed to caring for the environment and all creation. Wood Lake Publishing recycles, reuses, and encourages readers to do the same. Resources are printed on 100% post-consumer recycled paper and more environmentally friendly groundwood papers (newsprint), whenever possible. A percentage of all profit is donated to charitable organizations.

**Library and Archives Canada**
**Cataloguing in Publication**
McGinnis, Ray
Writing the sacred: a psalm-inspired path to appreciating and writing sacred poetry/Ray McGinnis.
Includes bibliographical references and index.
ISBN 1-896836-73-9
ISBN 13: 978-1-896836-73-7
1. Devotional poetry – Authorship. 2. Bible. O.T. Psalms – Devotional use. I. Title.
PN1042.M32 2005    808.1    C2005-900786-9

Published by Northstone
An imprint of Wood Lake Publishing Inc.
9590 Jim Bailey Road, Kelowna, BC, Canada, V4V 1R2
www.woodlakebooks.com
250.766.2778

Reprinted in 2007, 2009
Printing 10 9 8 7 6 5 4 3
Printed in Canada by
Transcontinental

## PERMISSIONS

The author has made every effort to trace the ownership of all copyrighted materials in this work and believes that all necessary permissions have been secured. If any errors or omissions have inadvertently been made, proper corrections will gladly be made in future editions.

Thanks are due to the following authors and publishers for permission to use the material included.

Unless otherwise indicated, all quotations from the Psalms are from *Songs for the Holy One: Psalms and Refrains for Worship,* by Thomas Barnett and Donald Patriquin. Kelowna, BC: Wood Lake Books Inc., 2004. Psalm texts copyright © 2004 Thomas Barnett. Used by permission of the publisher.

Scripture quotations from the *New Revised Standard Version,* copyright 1989 by the Division of Christian Education of the National Council of Churches of Christ in the USA. All rights reserved. Used by permission.

Quotations marked (NEB) are from the New English Bible with Apocrypha. Samuel Sandmel, ed. New York: Oxford University Press, 1976.

Quotations marked (NTP) are from *The New Testament and Psalms: An Inclusive Version.* Victor Roland Gold, ed. New York and London: Oxford University Press Inc., 1995.

Excerpts from "My Worst Habit" and "This Guest House" copyright 1995, 1997 translated by Coleman Barks. Reprinted from *The Essential Rumi,* HarperSanFrancisco and Castle Books, 1997 edition. Permission rights are given by Coleman Barks and Maypop Books, 196 Westview Drive, Athens, GA 30606.

Psalm 22, Psalm 33, Psalm 98, from *Opening to You,* by Norman Fischer, copyright © 2002 by Norman Fischer. Used by permission of Viking Penguin, a division of Penguin Group (USA) Inc.

"Even to This" is reprinted from *Poetic Medicine: The Healing Art of Poem-making* by John Fox, published by Jeremy P. Tarcher, Inc., 1997. Copyright © 1997 by John Fox with permission of the author.

Excerpt from Psalm 21 of Nan Merrill's *Psalms for Praying: An Invitation to Wholeness,* Copyright © 1996 by Nan C. Merrill. Reprinted by permission of The Continuum International Publishing Group.

Three quotations as submitted [81., 61., 41.] from *A Book of Psalms: Selected and Adapted from the Hebrew* by Stephen Mitchell. Copyright © 1993 by Stephen Mitchell. Reprinted by permission of HarperCollins Publishers Inc.

"Source of Time and Space," by Rabbi Zalman Schachter-Shalomi was originally written for *Prayers for a Thousand Years,* edited by Elizabeth Roberts and Elias Amidon, published by HarperSanFrancisco, 1999. Copyright © 1999. Rabbi Zalman Schachter-Shalomi retains copyright for this material and is reprinted with permission of the author.

Excerpts from "The Way It Is" and "A Ritual to Read to One Another" Copyright 1960, 1998 by the Estate of William Stafford. Reprinted from *The Way It Is: New & Selected Poems* with the permission of Graywolf Press, Saint Paul, Minnesota.

"What makes you sure?" reprinted from *(alive): Selected and new poems* by Rhea Tregebov, Wolsak and Wynn Publishers Ltd, 2004, by permission from the author and the publisher.

# Contents

Acknowledgments – **7**

Introduction – **9**

**CHAPTER 1:** At a Psalm-writing Workshop – **13**

**CHAPTER 2:** Psalms of Creation – **41**

**CHAPTER 3:** Psalms of Thanksgiving and Praise – **51**

**CHAPTER 4:** Psalms of Lament – **59**

**CHAPTER 5:** Psalms of Confession – **67**

**CHAPTER 6:** Psalms of Trust and Confidence – **75**

**CHAPTER 7:** Psalms of Wisdom – **81**

**CHAPTER 8:** Historical Psalms – **93**

**CHAPTER 9:** Vows in Psalms – **105**

**CHAPTER 10:** Royal Psalms – **115**

**CHAPTER 11:** Psalms for Holding a Vision – **127**

**CHAPTER 12:** New Psalms and other Sacred Poems – **137**

Epilogue – **189**

**APPENDIX A:** The Hebrew Psalms and
Literature of the Ancient Near East – **191**


**APPENDIX B:** The Influence of the Psalms in Jewish
and Christian Communities – **203**


**APPENDIX C:** The Psalms and other Religious Traditions – **211**


**APPENDIX D:** Notes on Pre-Columbian Literature
and the Psalm to Quetzalcoatl – **221**


Index of Scripture
and Other Sacred Writings – **223**

# Acknowledgments

This book would not have been possible without my mother, Alice, who taught me patience and a curiosity for sacred writings; and my father, Doug, who taught me fairness and accuracy. To Lois Huey-Heck and Tim Scorer who helped birth the idea of this book, I offer my gratitude. To Mike Schwartzentruber for his editorial guidance, my thanks. To Kathleen Adams who encouraged me on a path into the world of writing, and to Anne Michaels who rekindled a love of poetry, my grateful thanks. And to all who have helped me along the way to encounter the Source, you know who you are.

# *Introduction*

In his book *The Great Code,* Northrop Frye argues that the Bible is a key to understanding Western culture and the Western worldview. To *not* know that code is to be handicapped even in this age of technology. The literature found within the Bible is present, either directly or indirectly, in countless ways in movies, song lyrics, children's literature, and in the laws that govern Western society. In our post-modern era, different threads from our past come together in unexpected ways.

Several years ago, I saw Gabriel Axel's movie *Babette's Feast.* The storyline features a woman who was once a famous cook at a restaurant in Paris, but who now finds herself on the desolate coastline of Denmark. In need of work, she takes a job with two elderly religious women, as their housekeeper and cook. She is taught only to prepare boiled codfish and ale-bread soup. One day she wins 10,000 francs and decides to spend it on a magnificent meal, which she prepares for the simple villagers who are friends of the two women. Although the villagers are determined not to comment on the mouth-watering feast they are eating, a military officer who is at the dinner table concludes his compliments to the French cook by quoting from Psalm 85:10. "Love and fidelity have come together; justice and peace have joined hands."

The scriptwriter drew from the Psalms the climax to this story of an amazing feast. Within the context of the story itself, the quotation would have been recognizable to the simple religious villagers. The verse expresses what they have experienced in a language and world of meaning they can accept. For the late 20th-century audience, the insertion of this verse underscores the impression that the villagers in the movie have received a blessing, a lesson in the gift of hospitality, and reconciliation with the past.

The Psalms come from a distant place in time, written from the late 10th century BCE to the early 2nd century BCE. They are both beautiful and raw, menacing and inspired in their content. In them, we may discover sides of ourselves that have lain dormant, waiting for expression, waiting for the words of the unknown psalmist within us to speak. The military officer in *Babette's Feast* is not portrayed as a religious person. He knows the realities of the world and likely fought in the Franco-Prussian War. Yet it is this man of the world who evokes the sacred words of Psalm 85 to make meaning of this one incredible night of feasting. The religious villagers had committed themselves not to say anything about the meal, but only to keep their mind on God. The officer reminds them that God is both present in the meal and at work in the world. This presence was awakened through the agency of someone they were inclined to think of as a foreigner.

*Writing the Sacred* is for all the types of people we encounter in *Babette's Feast*, who live among us today. It is for those who only want to do what is "right," and who may therefore feel shy about writing new psalms because they fear they can't match the quality of the Hebrew originals. It is for people who, like the officer in *Babette's Feast,* are steeped in harsh realities; and for strangers and foreigners, who are trying to find a language that can make meaning of their lives.

This book discusses the Psalms at length. While I refer to over 40 individual psalms, I am not concerned with translations of or revisions to the existing canon. A great number of books already comment on the beauty and meaning of the Hebrew Psalms. Instead, this book is about using the Psalms as a starting place from which we can explore the connections between writing, the sacred, and poetry.

John Butler Yeats once said that nothing is sacred. His intention in saying this, however, was to provoke an examination of the conscience of humanity. Yeats appealed to his readers to be awake to an ethical imperative. In the chapters that follow, I explore a range of themes that describe different aspects of our relationship with the Creator, and of our experience of living in the world. In hallowing our experience, we move toward the holy even as the holy moves toward us. "Writing the sacred," then, involves nurturing a greater intimacy between the human and the divine. As an act, it points to the roots of our being, to that place of unity and oneness that is the source of and basis for our common destiny.

Poetry is about being open to the possibilities inherent in language to stir feeling and imagination. *Sacred* poetry stirs our imaginations and our emotions to contemplate the source of life. This is poetry that sees the sacred in the ordinary. It is poetry that both challenges and affirms.

In the pages that follow, you will encounter gentle writing exercises that encourage you to stretch your imagination, to explore your own openness, to express your emotions, and to experiment with forms of language, however imperfectly. While many of us have an inner critic that harshly judges our writing, or any *attempt* we make to write, I invite you here to pay no attention and to simply begin.

To help you, I present the literary forms that are present in the Hebrew Psalms and invite you to try them out for yourself.

Many readers may be curious about the historical background of the Psalms, and about how they intersect with literary forms from other cultures and spiritual paths, beginning with the world of the ancient Near East. I have included a number of appendices that delve into these topics in significant detail.

In Chapter 12, I have collected over 30 new psalms and sacred poems by writers from a variety of spiritual and philosophical perspectives. I approached both seasoned writers, as well as people who had never been published and, in some cases, had never written much poetry prior to my invitation. As a result, the psalm-poems themselves range from rough to polished, concrete to abstract, ordinary to exotic. My intention was to gather a variety of voices – the novice and the professional, the skeptic and the disciple – as well as a range of religious viewpoints, including Islamic, Jewish, Christian, and post-Christian. While I knew some of the contributors personally, many others were recommended to me.

In every case, I have been graced by the incredible openness shown by the contributors and I have sought to honor the dignity of difference and the gift of self-expression each has brought.

In this sampling of new poems and new psalms, you will encounter viewpoints that resemble your own, as well as ones that don't. My desire to include a variety of religious perspectives meant that I had to open myself to other ancient forms of psalm and sacred poetry. The Psalms of the Household of Muhammad, for example, offer a world of devotional literature unique to the Islamic faith and some writers chose literary forms that resemble this style of psalm. Another writer composed in the style of the pre-Columbian, Aztec psalms. Others chose to write in contemporary poetic forms.

This sample of new writing, then, does not uniformly reflect all the comments I make about the different poetic devices found in the Hebrew Psalms. The process of writing within any literary form involves continuity and innovation, and this will be true for you, too, as you try your hand at writing your own psalms.

Ultimately, I hope you will view the chapter of newly created works not as an occasion for praise or criticism, but as an invitation. Often, as readers, we experience a sense of disquiet if we can't understand something readily. Yet poetry is art. Writing a psalm is art. As such, it reflects a creative process of experimentation and self-expression.

I invite you, therefore, to be curious and respectful of the unique world from which each writer has drawn in order to compose his or her new psalm or poem. From that place of curiosity, I encourage you to express your own unique voice. More than that, I encourage you to *use* your voice as a way of approaching the sacred. May you grow in relationship with the One who breathed life into you, and who has placed within you a spark of the divine fire.

# 1

## At a Psalm-writing Workshop

The Psalms, with a few exceptions, are not the voice of God addressing us. They are rather the voice of our own common humanity – gathered over a long period of time...a voice that continues to have amazing authenticity... It speaks about life the way it really is, for in those deeply human dimensions the same issues and possibilities persist.[1]

— WALTER BRUEGGEMANN

**The Way It Is** (*excerpt*)
There's a thread you follow. It goes among
things that change. But it doesn't change.
People wonder about what you are pursuing.
You have to explain about the thread.
But it is hard for others to see...

— WILLIAM STAFFORD[2]

Listen to my words, Holy One, consider my murmurings;
Hear my earnest plea, you, my Sovereign and my God.
It is to you I pray. Holy One, hear my voice in the morning.[3]

— PSALM 5:1–3A

The voice of the psalmist echoes across the ages with a cry for help. The cry is not uttered in vain. It is not addressed to just anyone who might be within hearing distance. The cry of the psalmist is addressed to the *divine,* to the Name above all other names, to God. The psalmist trusts that when morning prayers are said, "You will hear me." However, these few lines from Psalm 5 suggest a relationship between the psalmist and God that goes beyond a passive confidence that God will take action. The psalmist has a role to play: one of rousing God to remember. The psalmist asks God to listen to their words, to their inmost thoughts, and to "heed my cry for help." The relationship is not an occasional one. God is not an infrequent visitor. Nor is the psalmist undisciplined in cultivating this relationship with God. We learn that in the morning, every morning, this psalmist says prayers. And God's response each morning is to hear those prayers.

As a former leader of youth and young adult programs for the United Church of Canada, I became aware that many youth struggle when they try to communicate at a level deeper than the shallow, surface exchanges that make up the bulk of their conversation. Beyond the world of "fine" and "how's it going," lies a world of meaning they have difficulty accessing.

I often met these youth while I was organizing a conference or retreat-center program. Their participation at these events represented a time away, a break from the ordinary routines of life. In most cases, the life they had left behind for a weekend, week, or semester, was the legacy of our modern world – a world of competition, tasks, deadlines, increasing responsibility, and acceleration of the speed they were required to attend to life. Taking time out between school, college, part-time or full-time work, I was meeting new leaders who were choosing to live more deeply than on automatic pilot. These leaders trusted that beyond shopping, beyond the pub, beyond the busyness of overtime and split shifts, there exists a deeper meaning to life's mysteries.

To these retreats they brought their own experiences of success, failure, perfectionism, loss, adventure, love, betrayal, envy, loyalty, wisdom, beauty, sensuality, desire, doubt, belief, power, powerlessness, suffering, violence, and compassion. They wanted to find a way to make meaning of their lives, and to speak about the way it is. They came seeking a framework that would be strong enough to hold them in all their wildness and vulnerability. They wanted a framework for making meaning that could help them pay attention to their life in a way that would enable them to move into each new day with confidence and trust. There was a thread they were following toward greater awareness of their own feelings and thoughts and actions, and they wanted to anchor that awareness in a relationship with the One who had created them.

At these gatherings, it was the word heard through storytelling, music, singing, poetry, and prayer that most powerfully communicated and enabled them to give voice to this thread. Readings from the Psalms were often used, because the Psalms communicate from a place in the heart able to reach a wide spectrum of participants.

The challenge of finding authentic ways of expressing what we think and feel, and of revealing to the Holy One our joys, sorrows, dark nights of the soul, and our restoration, remains with us no matter what our age. Psalm-writing offers us one way to listen afresh to our experience in the present moment. While the spiritual moods and themes found in the Psalms can awaken us to our own story, writing *new* psalms can help us shed light on our contemporary situation, much like writing new prayers can.

Before trying to write a psalm, it is helpful to look more closely at the literary elements that can be found within the traditional psalms of the Bible.

## PARALLELISM

Parallelism is a literary device that frequently anchors a psalm. "In Hebrew, [this] means that the second line [or clause] repeats the structure of the first, either adding a new thought, or a directly opposite one. Quite frequently, the second line simply adds a new thought, without using parallel words."[4]

This does not mean that all the psalms are the same, of course. Within the overarching parallel structure, much diversity can be found because the authors of the psalms also employed a variety of other literary devices. These devices each have a name:[5] restatement, lists, citation, statement and question, questions, contrast and reversal, mixing of singular and plural, repetition of a word or a phrase, expansion or definition, and acrostic poems. By looking at the examples below, we can discover a range of possibilities as we start to write our own new psalms.

In the discussion that follows, ten different forms of writing within the Psalms are explored more fully. A suggested exercise follows the discussion of each technique or form. I encourage you to try out these exercises as you read, or to return to them when you feel ready. Having a notebook or journal at your side will enable you to jump into the heart of the writing process.

## LISTS

In many psalms, the writer includes short lists. Two or three phrases, similar in length, add a sense of momentum to the testimony of what is being done by God, or by the enemies of the people of God; or to a list of the things the people of God, or servant of God, have done. In the case of the psalm below, we find a list of what the psalmist is requesting from God:

> O my God, treat them like whirling dust,
>     like chaff before the wind,
>     like fire burning forests,
>     like flames destroying mountains,
> Destroy them with your tempest,
>     terrify them with your storms.
>
> — PSALM 83:13–15

In this psalm, the poet is on a roll. It is as if a list has been made of all the things the psalmist wants God to do. This example from Psalm 83 can raise ethical issues for us. Do we want God to hunt down our enemies, like a raging fire or a windstorm? And yet who has not, in a moment of hurt or fear, wished something could happen to make our adversaries run for the hills. In this case, the psalmist makes it clear, in verse 16, that his purpose in asking for these things is "so that they may seek your name, Most High."

Lists occur in many sacred and secular writings. The Muslim writer of the *Ganjul Arsh*, from India, has essentially created a list as he ascribes particular qualities to different prophets in the Muslim teaching.

Adam the Chosen One of God
  Noah the Delivered One of God
Abraham the Friend of God
  Ishmael the Sacrifice of God
Moses the Confidant of God
  David the Caliph of God
'Isa the Spirit of God
  Muhammad the Apostle of God...[6]

Making lists is something we do often. We make lists of chores to do, groceries to buy, places to visit, plans for the year ahead, charities to donate to, activities to include at a party for an anniversary, birthday, or celebration. In her book *Simple Abundance*, Sarah Ban Breathnach invites journal writers to list, at the end of each day, the things they are thankful for. I kept this practice for five years, making a list of five things I was thankful for at the close of the day. I included these five things in a verse which, looking at it now, I realize falls within the literary form of a parallelism.

Thank you, O God, for this amazing day
  for sailboats, wind and water
for blue skies and majestic white clouds
  stretching across the horizon.

*Exercise:* Experiment with the "list" parallelism. Let's start by working with the theme of thankfulness. Make a short list of things you are thankful to God for. Express this in two or three lines that build upon each other.

## RESTATEMENT

Another way in which parallelism is used in the Psalms is through restatement. In restatement, a phrase is not repeated, but restated. For example:

Praise the Holy One from the heavens!
  Sing praises in the heights above!

— Psalm 148:1

In both phrases, the psalmist praises God, first in the heavens, and then in the heights.

This use of parallelism is also found in the pre-Columbian literature of Mexico. Restating the same thought twice in succeeding parallel lines, an Aztec poem of praise to the Sun, Huitzilopochtli, includes these lines:

> From where eagles are resting,
> from where the tigers are exalted...[7]

Here the Aztec poem makes clear that other species are blessed by what the Sun does, and so eagles may rest and tigers thrive in daylight.

*Exercise:* Write a statement to God and then restate it in a second phrase.

## CITATION

In a number of psalms, the poet uses quotes to create a sense of dialogue between God and the psalmist, or between the psalmist and other friends or adversaries. In Psalm 41, each unit builds to enhance the dialogue, as in verses 4–5:

> Finally I said, "Holy One, have mercy on me.
>    Heal my soul, for I have sinned against you."
> My enemies cruelly mutter against me,
>    "When will he die, and his name perish?"

> — PSALM 41:4–5

When this device of citation is introduced into a psalm, it creates a live conversation. When psalms are read aloud, citing the words of different partners in a dialogue can be engaging, whether the focus is consolation or disagreement. In this example, the whole parallelism is devoted to quotation. In other cases, the citation comprises only one half of a specific parallelism:

I say to you, my rock,
  "Why have you forgotten me?"

— Psalm 42:9

*Exercise:* Write several lines that introduce quotes from one voice, or from two partners, to create a sense of live dialogue.

## STATEMENT AND QUESTION

In other psalms, statement and question are used together to add variety to the units of lines and phrases in each parallelism.

My bones say, "O God,
  who is like you?
  You deliver the weak from those with
  too much power,
  the poor and weak from
  their despoilers."

— Psalm 35:10

The combination of questions and statements can shape the rhythm of the psalm. A question often evokes a thought which may cause the reader to ponder, for a moment, the question asked. The statement picks up the tempo after the question has been posed.

This literary technique is found in other poetic writing, such as this coupling from the poem *My Worst Habit,* written in the 13th century by the Persian poet Jelaluddin Rumi.

How to cure bad water?
  Send it back to the river.
How to cure a bad habit?
  Send me back to you.

— Rumi[8]

*Exercise:* Write several statements and questions that point out something you want God to know, or something you are wondering about God.

## QUESTIONS

In other psalms, the parallelism consists only of questions.

> O God, why have you utterly rejected us?
> Why does your anger burn
> > against the sheep in your pasture?
>
> — PSALM 74:1

> Who is God
> and where is God,
> of whom is God,
> and where his dwelling?...
> Is He in heaven
> or on the earth?
> In the sea,
> in the rivers,
> in the mountains,
> in the valleys?
> > — THE QUESTIONS OF ETHNE ALBA (7TH CENTURY, IRELAND)[9]

Questions have an impact on the hearer. Usually, they elicit an answer or an inquiry into the question raised. Sometimes, the response to a question is another question. Whatever the question, the standard conversational response is to pay attention, consider the question, and respond. The impact of posing a series of questions is to increase the sense of urgency. It can again shift the mood of the psalm, driving the reader deeper into wonder, lament, or other emotions as they wrestle with God.

*Exercise:* Write several lines each beginning with the word "why."

Of course, it is possible to mix it up a bit by using other words, such as how, what, who, does, and when, to start a question. But by using the same word repeatedly at the start of each phrase for emphasis, a rhythm builds for both the speaker and the hearer of the psalm.

## Contrast and Reversal

Another device or variation found within parallelism is contrast and reversal. Here, the first statement is followed by a second, which either demonstrates a marked contrast to the first statement, or creates the effect of a sharp u-turn from the message in the first line or phrase. The first example, below, comes from the Book of Lamentations; the second from the Book of Psalms.

> Those who once fed delicately
> > are desolate in the streets,
> and those who nurtured in purple
> > now grovel on dunghills.
>
> > – Lamentations 4:5 (NEB)

In the next two verses of Psalm 49, the reversal is unmistakable.

> Do not fear when some become rich,
> > and their wealth increases,
> > for at death they cannot take it with them,
> > and their possessions will not follow them.
>
> > – Psalm 49:16–17

In the sensual Song of Songs, contrast and reversal are employed through the voice of the bride, who hears that her lover has come to knock at her door.

> I have stripped off my dress,
> > must I put it on again?
> I have washed my feet,
> > must I soil them again?
>
> > – Song of Songs 5:3 (NEB)

In this instance, the poet uses two poetic devices simultaneously. One is contrast and reversal: strip off dress/put it on; washed my feet/must I soil them. The second device is alternating statements and questions, discussed on previous pages.

New Christian communities created hymns, poems, and prayers that borrowed their style from the Psalms. One example of the freedom early Christians found in composing new sacred poetry can be found in The Books of Hymns, from the Dead Sea Scrolls. Here is my paraphrase of that early Christian psalm.

> **You Bear Me Comfort, O Lord**
> You bear me comfort, O Lord... amid the sadness of grief.
> You bear me words of peace in the midst of devastation.
> You bear me dauntlessness of heart when I fade.
> You bear me courage in the face of distress.
> You brought me ease of speech when my lips faltered.
> You brought me endurance and power when my spirit
>    languished.
> You brought my feet to stand secure when they stood where
>    cruelty is crowned.
> I am only a faint image, but for those who turn around,
> I am a source of wholeness.
>
> – BOOK OF HYMNS 2:3–5[10]

Here the poet addresses the divine using contrast and reversal. In my paraphrase, the contrast consists of naming different things God has provided in the context of the relationship: comfort where there was sadness, peace where there was devastation, dauntlessness where one was fading, courage where there was distress, ease of speech where there were halting lips, endurance and power where there was a languishing spirit, and a source of wholeness from a faint image.

What contrasts do you notice around you? What does God seem to be showing you about life? The young grow old, the healthy get sick, the happy suffer, those who grieve rejoice again, those who were fatigued renew their strength.

Life is full of reversals. When we bring to God our awareness of reversals, it can give us perspective and increase our wisdom about how to view life. The famous hymn *Amazing Grace* contains the line, "I once was lost, but now I'm found, was blind, but now I see." The lyric draws upon the essence of literary contrast and reversal, which we meet in the Psalms.

*Exercise:* Make a list of contrasts or reversals you have experienced or observed in the following situations.

What contrasts or reversals have you experienced in your life?

What contrasts of reversals have you observed in the lives of those around you?

What contrasts or reversals are you aware of in nature?

What contrasts or reversals are you aware of in the lives of other peoples and nations (such as famine, war, prosperity, peace)?

### Singular and Plural

In other line couplings within the Psalms, the poet alters the singular and plural, when referring to the subject in the line. While we constantly use singular and plural in our daily conversation, for some people these literary terms pose a challenge. So here is a refresher for the busy person who may have forgotten what these terms refer to.

|  | **Singular** | **Plural** |
|---|---|---|
| **First Person** | I, me, my | us, we, our |
| **Second Person** | you | you |
| **Third Person** | he, she | them, they |

Better is a little that the righteous person has,
    than the abundance of many wicked.

> – Psalm 37:16 (NRSV)

Here the righteous in the first line is referred to in the third person singular, but the wicked (them) in the second line are referred to in the third person plural. This poetic technique can create a sense of contrast or surprise for the hearer as they adjust to the change from a singular to plural focus. Another variation on this is to change the focus from the first, second, or third person within the singular or plural.

> While the king was on his couch,
>      my nard gave forth its fragrance.
>
> — Song of Songs 1:12 (NRSV)

Making the subject in the first line different than the subject in the second line informs the hearer about what else is going on. In the quotation from the Song of Songs above, the focus in line one is on the king (third person singular), while the second line is focused on the speaker, through the use of the first person singular "my." This is not just a psalm about one person, but compares or contrasts their situation with another or others, friend or foe.

Using both singular and plural is a literary device that is not limited to the Hebrew Bible. In this old English nursery rhyme, the shift is made from first person singular to second person singular:

> Lavender blue, dilly-dilly,
>      lavender green
> When I am king, dilly-dilly
>      You'll be my queen.

In the third line, the focus is on the first person singular: I. The fourth line switches attention to the second person singular: you. This simple change introduces novelty for the hearer of the verse, inviting them to notice the shift in the subject of the poet's attention.

*Exercise:* Experiment with shifting from first person to second or third person, or from singular to plural by completing the following sentence stem couplings:

1. I...
   But you...

2. They...
   While we...

3. She...
   However, for them...

## REPETITION OF A WORD OR A PHRASE

One way to draw the hearer into a psalm is to emphasize a word or a phrase by repeating it in following line. This is different from restatement, where the second half of the coupling provides a twist with new imagery, compared to the first line. A careful look at the two lines below reveals that the word "aloud" in the first line is omitted in the second line. In the breadth of the Psalms, "repetition" includes both full repetition and partial repetition. In Psalm 77 the psalmist tells us,

> I cried aloud to God,
>    I cried to God, and God heard me.
>                                — PSALM 77:1 (NEB)

By repeating the phrase "I cried to God," the hearer knows that this is important. There is nothing casual about the psalmist's disclosure. Something is happening here that is important to the psalmist – so important that they repeat it to drive the message home.

Repetition also serves to provide a rhythm, which in some cases mirrors the topic that is being discussed. In Psalm 93, the poet uses the phrase "the ocean lifts up."

> O God, the ocean lifts up,
>    the ocean lifts up its clamor;
> the ocean lifts up its pounding waves.
>                                — PSALM 93:3 (NEB)

The repetition of the phrase builds as the poet adds the emotional description of clamor. The third line in this tricolon gives a detailed description of what the poet can see: pounding waves. In the 1960s, the pop group Herman's Hermits repeated the title of their hit *I'm Henry the Eighth I Am,* over and over again throughout the song. The use of repetition can serve to create a refrain that repeats not just in one parallel coupling of lines, but in a series of verses. It is possible that this psalm was designated for two parts, a leader and a congregation, with the congregation reciting the second part of each pairing within the verse.

> Praise the Holy One, who is so good,
>> whose faithful love endures forever!
> Let the house of Israel proclaim,
>> "God's faithful love endures forever!"
> Let the house of Aaron say,
>> "God's faithful love endures forever!"
> Let all who revere the Holy One say,
>> "God's faithful love endures forever!"

– PSALM 118:1–4

As the repetition builds in Psalm 118, the hearer is invited to agree more and more emphatically that God's love endures forever. As the mind focuses on this thought, something may occur for the speaker and the hearer. For a moment, we may find ourselves encouraged by the idea that God's love endures forever. Where we may have felt irritation, sadness, confusion, fear or anxiety, our mind has shifted to this affirmation of God's lasting love. A spiritual mystery is afoot as we recite this psalm.

*Exercise:* Using the repeated line from Psalm 118, create new phrases while continuing to alternate them with the phrase "God's love endures forever." Create whatever statement or question you wish with this alternating phrase. The pattern should look like this.

A) _____

B) God's love endures forever.

*Exercise:* Now invent your own phrase and repeat it through two verses.

## EXPANSION, OR DEFINITION

Another poetic device found in the Psalms is the use of echo, expansion of thought, or introduction of information that defines or clarifies the first line in the coupling. The tone of the second line can vary greatly. Sometimes it echoes the first line.

> The storm sank to a murmur,
>> and the waves of the sea were stilled.
>
> — PSALM 107:29 (NEB)

Other times, the subsequent lines simply expand the thought in the first line.

> Like a lengthening shadow,
>> I am fading away,
>> shaken off like a locust.
> My knees collapse from hunger,
>> the fat has wasted from my body.
>
> — PSALM 109:23–24

Still, in other instances, the subsequent line has a defining or clarifying effect.

> I love God, because God has heard my voice
>> and my supplications;
> Because God listened to me,
>> therefore I will call on God as long as I live.
>
> — PSALM 116:1–2 (NTP)

Within many psalms, the poet plays with these different devices drawing the hearer in.

This same technique has been used in many popular songs over the ages. For example, in *O Susanna,* which Stephen Foster penned in the mid-1800s, a sequence of information is given in succeeding lines. The protagonist comes from Alabama. He has a banjo on his knee. He's going to Louisiana, where he'll see his true love. Foster then employs contrast and reversal, stating that it rained all night, yet the weather was dry; and that the heat of the sun nearly froze the protagonist to death. By filling out the details, Foster creates a picture full of paradox, while expanding on the story.

*Exercise:* Write several verses expanding or defining or clarifying information in the first line or phrase of each verse.

## ACROSTIC: ALPHA-POEM

One of the more distinctive variants of poetic verse found in the Hebrew Psalms is the acrostic device. In an acrostic psalm, each of the verses, or half-verses, begins with a successive letter in the Hebrew alphabet, which consists of 22 letters. Notations in many modern Bibles identify Psalms 34, 111, and 119 as using this acrostic style of writing.[11] Unfortunately, English translations are not able to reflect this device.

Below is an acrostic poem using the letters of the English alphabet. As this alphabet has 26 letters, there are 26 lines. Notice that once a word starting with the next letter in the alphabet is brought to mind, the poem drops down a line, continuing in this way through the whole alphabet. For practical purposes, the letter **X** and the letter **Z** can be replaced with words that are phonetically similar. For example, words with the sound of the consonant **X** in the first syllable – such as a**x**e, e**x**cite, o**x**ygen, o**x**en or u**x**orious – can be inserted in the 24th line of the acrostic. For **Z**, try please or easy! To start an acrostic or alpha-poem, the poet has to have in mind a word beginning with the letter **A**. Here are a number of words starting with the letter **A**, which I considered before I began to write my acrostic psalm: *a, abide, accept, acclaim, after, allow, almighty, alone, among, an, any, are, arise, as, at, attend, awake...*

All day long my heart praises You, O God;

before I rise You are there to greet me.

Comfort me when I am in distress;

declare to me You are not finished with me yet.

Even when my heart is

faint, I remember the

God of my salvation.

Hallelujahs fill my voice;

I find once more the strength to praise You.

Justice and mercy sit at your side;

keep me safe from harm, the arrows of the gossip.

Loving God, how can I thank You; You who are

merciful and wondrous.

No one can match your power

or sway You from Your righteous ways.

Prepare me for the days to come;

question me and search me that I may be well,

rejoice in You, and be glad.

Save me from myself, my desperate thoughts;

tenderly You hold me, like a mother hen her chicks.

Unto You I count all my blessings, so

very gracious are you, supporting me every day,

Waking or sleeping. You

eXtend Your love near and far;

young lions roar in praise of Your name, and like

Zebras grazing in grasslands, I am warmed by your sun.

*Exercise:* Try writing your own acrostic psalm. I used the English alphabet in the example above. If your first language uses a different alphabet, feel free to use it instead.

As you prepare to write your poem, consider what word of thanks, lament, praise, confession, trust, or wisdom you wish to include in your acrostic psalm. What do you want to express to God? What questions do you have for God? Do you want to write from the perspective of yourself as an individual, or from the view of a community (group of people, nation)? Or on behalf of the earth, animals, plants...

Once you have decided on the focus of your starting thought, open yourself to the possibility of writing something new. Know that what you write does not need to be perfect. We will address the issue of perfectionism later in this chapter. For now, allow a word starting with the letter **A** to drop into your consciousness. Allow yourself to experiment and write without judgment.

Once you have completed the above exercise, take a moment to re-read what you have just written. Complete the following lines:

I, _____, have written a psalm today.
   (your name)

As God is my witness, with the spirit moving within me, I can write whenever I choose!

Signature: _____  Date: _____

## MAKING POETIC CHOICES

In this chapter, ten different poetic devices have been explored. Each is an example of a poetic choice made by the writers of the Hebrew Psalms. A careful study of the Psalms would include more distinctions. For example, the use of simile, where one thing is compared to something else, is an evident device in the Psalms: "I am like a spreading olive tree in God's house" (Psalm 52:8). There are places in the Psalms where the poetic devices being employed are more obscure and the connections within a verse or between verses seem to create a full-stop effect. As 21st-century people, we can be critical of particular psalms, or wonder why they are included in The Book of Psalms. Psalm 117 seems to be a chorus or a refrain, but it is not particularly memorable when compared to Psalms 23 or 46, which represent literary high points.

In his discussion of the Psalms, James Kugel states that "biblical 'poetry' is a complex of heightening effects used in combinations and intensities that vary widely from composition to composition even within a single 'genre.'" He considers the concept of biblical poetry itself to be somewhat problematic. "[T]hat term will, if based on the various...features seen, include compositions whose genre and subject are most unpoetic by Western standards." So the idea of biblical poetry can "imply a structural regularity and design that are simply not there."[12] In other words, we need to take care that certain general observations about parallelism do not cloud our ability to see exceptions to the rule, both in the Hebrew Psalms, and in our own compositions.

Since the poetic choices we can make vary widely, we have some freedom to experiment. If a psalm were a salad, the poetic devices described in this chapter are some of the ingredients that would go into its making. But *we* are the ones who choose what to mix into our psalm salad. The amounts – one part restatement, two parts questioning, one part citation, and so on – are choices we make as we fashion a new creation. In the creative process of crafting a psalm, we also choose a focus to write about.

### Choosing a Theme: What Do I Want to Express to God?

In the Psalms, the direct expression of emotion powerfully communicates to those who read or hear the words. Whatever else the psalmists seek to express to God, they let God know how they are feeling. Read each of the following excerpts from the Psalms. It is good to read them aloud to let the words have their impact.

> I love You, O God, my strength.
>
> — Psalm 18:1 (NEB)

> I am weary from groaning.
>   every night I soak my bed with tears.
>   They drench my pillow.
>
> — Psalm 6:6

> Even though I walk through the darkest valley
>   I fear no evil; for you are with me;
> your rod and your staff – they comfort me.
>
> — Psalm 23:4 (NRSV)

Pay attention! Answer me!
My anxiety devastates me
    and I am driven to distraction by the enemy's clamor,
    the hostile pressure of the wicked.
They pile trouble upon me,
    venting their anger on me.
My heart quails within me;
    death's terrors assault me.
Fear and trembling assail me
    and horror overwhelms me.

– Psalm 55:2–5

My whole being yearns,
    aching for God's courts.
My body and soul shout with joy,
    joy in the living God.

– Psalm 84:2

As you read the verses from these selected psalms, what impact did you notice in your body, your heart, your mind? By speaking the language of emotion, the psalmist invites us into the realm of the heart. Direct expression of emotion invites understanding, sympathy, and possibly empathy. The psalmist invites us into a deeper intimacy of relationship with God, as the quality of emotion is expressed.

*Exercise:* Take a moment to look over the feelings listed below. Circle the ones that stand out for you now, because they reflect your current reality.

| | | | | | |
|---|---|---|---|---|---|
| afraid | absorbed | affectionate | aggravated | agitated | agony |
| alarmed | alert | alienated | alive | aloof | amazed |
| ambivalent | amused | angry | anguished | animated | animosity |
| annoyed | anxious | apathetic | appalled | appreciative | apprehensive |
| ardent | aroused | ashamed | astonished | aversion | awed |
| baffled | beat | bereaved | bewildered | blessed | blissful |

| | | | | | |
|---|---|---|---|---|---|
| bored | burnt out | calm | chagrined | clear-headed | cold |
| comfortable | confident | confused | contempt | content | compassionate |
| courage | cranky | curious | dazed | dazzled | disconnected |
| dejected | depleted | depressed | despair | despondent | disconcerted |
| detached | devastated | delighted | discouraged | disgruntled | disappointed |
| disgusted | dislike | dismayed | displeased | disquiet | disheartened |
| distant | distracted | disturbed | dreamy | discombobulated | |
| eager | ecstatic | edgy | elated | embarrassed | empowered |
| enchanted | encouraged | energetic | engaged | engrossed | enchanted |
| enlivened | enthralled | enthusiastic | entranced | enraged | exhilarated |
| expectant | exuberant | envious | exasperated | excited | exhausted |
| fascinated | fatigue | fidgety | flustered | foreboding | friendly |
| frightened | frustrated | fulfilled | fun | furious | giddy |
| glad | gloomy | grateful | guilty | happy | hate |
| hesitant | hopeful | hopeless | horrified | hostile | impatient |
| incensed | indifferent | indignant | irate | irked | irritated |
| insecure | inspired | interested | intrigued | invigorated | involved |
| jealous | jittery | joyful | jubilant | kind | lethargic |
| listless | lively | livid | lonely | lost | love |
| melancholy | mellow | miserable | mistrustful | mortified | mystified |
| nervous | nostalgic | numb | open | optimistic | overwhelmed |
| outraged | pain | panicked | passionate | petrified | perplexed |
| perturbed | pining | pleased | puzzled | quiet | radiant |
| rapturous | rattled | refreshed | regretful | rejuvenated | relaxed |
| relieved | remorseful | renewed | repulsed | resentful | rested |
| restless | restored | revived | sad | safe | satisfied |
| scared | secure | sensitive | serene | shocked | spellbound |
| startled | stressful | still | stimulated | surprised | suspicious |
| sympathetic | tender | tense | terrific | thankful | thrilled |
| tickled | torn | tranquil | troubled | trusting | turbulent |
| turmoil | understood | uneasy | unhappy | uninterested | uncomfortable |
| unnerved | unsettled | upset | vibrant | vulnerable | warm |
| wary | weary | wistful | withdrawn | wonder | wonderful |
| worried | wretched | yearning | youthful | zealous | |

***Exercise:*** Look at the feeling words you have circled on the previous page. Of these, choose five that suggest themselves to you most strongly. Write those five feelings down on the next line:

_____

Fill in the following sentences below. Choose a different feeling for each of these five sentences and consider what you want to let God know when you feel this way. What can you let God know about what this feeling seems to be communicating? What opportunity does experiencing this feeling offer you to draw closer to God?

When I feel _____ I want to express to God _____
      (1ST FEELING)

And when I feel _____ I want God to know _____
      (2ND FEELING)

And when I feel _____ I want to ask God _____
      (3RD FEELING)

And when I feel _____ I long for God to _____
      (4TH FEELING)

And when I feel _____ I seek from God _____
      (5TH FEELING)

## CLEARING A PATH TO WRITE A NEW PSALM

In her book *The Seven Whispers: Listening to the Voice of Spirit,* Christina Baldwin writes a dialogue with God. She calls it a "Godalogue."[13] Writing a dialogue with God invites us into an honest relationship with God about what is happening in our lives – our context, the challenges we face, the grace we have received. If you are still reading this book, you are likely preparing to write a new psalm. You may not trust yourself as a writer yet, but you at least have an interest in awakening your writing ability. And you have already done this once, if you tried to write an acrostic alpha-poem in the exercise earlier in the chapter. So let's clear a path that will enable you to give yourself full permission to write.

*Exercise:* Write down five things that your inner critic may say to you about your writing that would discourage you from writing a new psalm. For example:

- What if my psalm is boring?
- I don't know if I have anything original to express.
- The Psalms are so wonderful. I could paraphrase one of the original 150 psalms, but I could never write anything that could compare with them.
- I feel like a fraud. Who am I to have a relationship with God?
- I really want to write, it's just that when I was nine years old my teacher told me I wasn't any good at it.

Once you have written the five statements your inner critic or judge is likely to make, you can write your Godalogue bringing these obstacles to your written conversation with the Creator.

Here is part of the dialogue I wrote in my Godalogue.

**Me:**  God, I'm not sure I'm the right person to be writing this book on the Psalms. I haven't got a master's degree in theology. I don't read Hebrew. Maybe I'm in over my head.

**God:**  Hello, Ray. I've heard this kind of talk from you before. It is an old voice, a voice you don't need to pay attention to anymore. How long are you going to tell yourself that you haven't studied enough, or received enough degrees to qualify to write this project?

**Me:**  Good question. It's as if I get excited about a new project and then I step back. I know I have been raised on the Psalms from my upbringing in church. I know many psalms from melodies I have learned, and there are several that have been especially important on my spiritual journey.

**God:**  Sounds like you have these psalms in your blood.

**Me:**  So you think I have enough to jump into this project?

**God:**  Of course you do. Look, I created you. You have the ability to research a topic. Once you dive in, you listen to the wisdom that emerges as you create, shape, and imagine the design of the manuscript. And besides, what have you been doing these last five years?

**Me:** Teaching writing, creative journal writing, prayer writing, and poetry workshops. So what do you think my hesitation is about?

**God:** Just failure. Look, more than half the people I have created fear failure. The fact that you don't want to put energy into creating something that is mediocre or that misses the mark is understandable.

**Me:** Bingo. I have a streak of perfectionism in me and so I worry I'll spend all this time writing. I worry that I won't know if I have produced a masterpiece or simply deserve a "good try" ribbon. It's like when I was in grade nine writing an English essay. Before I handed in the paper, I found it hard to judge whether I was really on to something or had missed the whole point of the assignment.

**God:** Did I ever tell you to just be still?

**Me:** Yes, God.

**God:** Well, being still requires that you let your mind slow down. What happens when you don't take time to breathe?

**Me:** I look at a project that I haven't started and feel overwhelmed. It's only when I remember that I can look at the different parts of the assignment that I find the project both interesting and manageable.

**God:** So write out a list of all the ideas and possibilities for this book on the Psalms that you are going to write. Then circle five simple tasks that you would be willing to try. Of those five, circle the one you will commit to, starting today.

**Me:** You surprise me with how practical you can be sometimes, being the mystery that you are.

**God:** I AM who I AM.

*Exercise:* Now, using the Godalogue, bring before God your insecurities, worries, concerns, lack of trust or confidence, judgment or resistance to writing a new psalm. Tackle one or more of the critical voices inside you and bring them before the God who created, knows, and loves you. Allow God to rebut or express anything you need to hear in order to be able to move forward. Let God speak a word that will help you write a new psalm to God. In this Godalogue, you write both parts. Allow 15 to 20 minutes to express your concerns, and then listen for God's reply. You and God can make any statement or pose any question to each other in the Godalogue.

Begin by taking a moment to be still.

Allow yourself to be open to the presence of God.

Breathe.

Know that God is near.

Decide who will begin the Godalogue: you or God.

When you are ready, one of you can begin by saying hello.

Write down everything that comes to you in this Godalogue.

Keep writing until you and God have reached a satisfying place in your conversation.

## ADDRESSING THE DIVINE

A common feature of the Psalms is that they address the divine by name in the first few verses. In the New Revised Standard Version of the Bible, the divine name is often rendered or translated as God and Lord. On fewer occasions, God is referred to as Most High, Creator, shepherd of Israel, almighty, rock, king, and ruler. Oxford biblical scholar Victor Roland Gold explains some of the choices that were made by English translators of the Psalms.

> The two most common names for God in the Hebrew Bible are *Yahweh* and *Elohim*... *Elohim* is always translated as "God," and *Yahweh* as "Lord," in the NRSV. *Yahweh* does not properly mean Lord; "the one who causes to come into existence" or a similar phrase would be more accurate. Lord is a convention adopted by the Jews probably in order to avoid pronouncing the divine name, which they regarded as sacred. (Using) "God" for *Yahweh* and "God" for *Elohim* (is an acceptable convention). On occasion, *Yahweh* is rendered as Creator – probably closer to the original meaning of the name.[14]

A wide range of images for God can be found within the scope of the Hebrew Bible and the New Testament. In the Qur'an, there are 99 beautiful names for God. The point that I want to underscore here is that the names by which we might address the Holy One have not been exhausted. For each name for God that we have received from tradition, there was a time in history when that name was new and emerged within a particular culture or community. As each new generation enters the living tradition of the God who told Moses "I Am who I Am," it can open itself to the leading of spirit and imagining new names for the divine. The appeal of our imagination will ultimately be tested within a wider community that makes use of the name in their faith life, or not.

Zen-Buddhist writer Stephen Mitchell comments that writing within a particular language holds possibilities and limitations. In the case of English, he says that addressing God presents some practical challenges, "...because English lacks a personal pronoun to express what includes and transcends both genders."[15] Mitchell points out that the eighth-century Chinese writer Lao-tzu, writing within his own linguistic tradition, was not presented with the same dilemma. Consequently, in order to be faithful to the original, English translations of Lao-tzu's writing must render God using neutral pronouns.

> There was something formless and perfect
> before the universe was born.
> It is serene. Empty.
> Solitary. Unchanging.
> Infinite. Eternally present.
> It is the mother of the universe.
> For lack of a better name,
> I call it the Tao.[16]

For followers of any spiritual path in China, this makes sense, because there is no masculine or feminine pronoun in Chinese for the divine. The evolution of the world's major languages is a fascinating area of study, though it is one that far exceeds the scope of this book. However, even a cursory glimpse into that world of study can inspire us to rethink the language we use for the Name above all other Names. Using masculine and feminine imagery for God holds rich possibilities for English speaking peoples. Yet it is a surprise for many to encounter the freedom that is available to those whose languages do not use masculine and feminine pronouns for God. As you write a psalm, consider how you wish to address the Holy.

For numbers of people, the term God has not been helpful in their spiritual journey. Sam Keen, in his book *Hymn to an Unknown God*, writes of that "nameless separation that divides us from our world and from ourselves." He comments, "the search to determine whether there is any reality that answers to the names of spirit, soul, or God can only be a passionate existential journey to discover the deepest meaning of being a person."[17] For readers who find God language problematic but who wish to try the exercises in this book, I invite you to use language that fits your own authentic spiritual expression. For some, terms such as "presence," "inner wisdom," "light," or "love," may speak more powerfully. There is mystery in what unites, binds, and draws us to one another. I invite you to write mindful of whatever you think holds the world together.

## A Word about Simile and Metaphor

As poetic cousins, simile and metaphor are often confused. If I write "a good poem is like a good conversation," I'm using a simile. I'm suggesting a good poem may be as enjoyable as a good conversation. If I write "a good poem is a good conversation" I'm not comparing poetry with conversation. I'm using metaphor by suggesting they can be viewed as equal. For a lover of poetry, the best "conversation" may come from poems. Metaphors are used to equate something. Similes point to things resembling each other. Similes in the Psalms include "I am like an olive tree in the house of the Holy One" (Psalm 52:8), and "When the Holy One restores Zion's fortunes, it will be like a glorious dream" (Psalm 126:1). And in Psalm 125 the writer says that God's care is like the hills over Jerusalem. As and like alert us to the use of simile. Browse through the Psalms. What similes you can find?

### Exercise: Using Similes

Consider your relationship with the Divine. How does it resemble something in nature? Is it like the hills over Jerusalem, or an olive tree or...?

### Exercise: Using Metaphors

"The Lord is my shepherd" (Psalm 23:1, NRSV) and "The Holy One is my light and my saving help..." (Psalm 27:1) show the strength of metaphor. Consider your relationship with the Creator. What is God for you on your spiritual journey? Complete the phrase "God is..."

The next chapters explore the variety of themes found in the Psalms – themes to explore as we expand our own relationship with God.

## ENDNOTES

[1] Walter Brueggemann, *Praying the Psalms* (Winona, Minnesota: St. Mary's Press, 1986), 16–17.

[2] William Stafford, *The Way It Is* (St. Paul, Minnesota: Greywolf Press, 1998), 42.

[3] Unless otherwise indicated, all quotations from the Psalms are from Thomas Barnett and Donald Patriquin, *Songs for the Holy One* (Kelowna, BC: Wood Lake Books, 2004).

[4] Thomas Barnett, prologue to *Songs for the Holy One* (Kelowna, BC: Wood Lake Books, 2004).

[5] James L. Kugel, *The Idea of Biblical Poetry* (New Haven: Yale Univesity Press, 1981), 1–95.

[6] Constance E. Padwick, *Muslim Devotions* (Oxford, England: Oneworld Publications, 1996), 168.

[7] Miguel León-Portilla, *Pre-Columbian Literature of Mexico* (Norman, Oklahoma: University of Oklahoma, 1969), 77.

[8] Coleman Barks, *The Essential Rumi* (Edison, New Jersey: Castle Books, 1997), 52.

[9] P. Murray, ed., *The Deer's Cry: A Treasury of Irish Religious Verse* (Dublin: Four Courts Press, 1986), 15.

[10] For an original translation of the "Book of Hymns," see Theodore Gastor, *The Dead Sea Scriptures in English Translation* (New York: Doubleday, 1976), 148.

[11] Samuel Sandmel, ed., *The New English Bible with the Apocrypha,* Oxford Study Edition (New York: Oxford University Press, 1976), 650.

[12] Kugel, *Biblical Poetry,* 94.

[13] Christina Baldwin, *The Seven Whispers: Listening to the Voice of Spirit* (Novato, California: New World Library, 2002), 31–32.

[14] Victor Roland Gold, ed., *The New Testament and Psalms: An Inclusive Version* (New York: Oxford University Press, 1995), xxi.

[15] Stephen Mitchell, *A Book of Psalms: Selected and Adapted from the Hebrew* (New York: HarperCollins, 1993), xiv.

[16] Ibid.

[17] Sam Keen, *Hymn to an Unknown God* (New York and Toronto: Bantam Books, 1994), xxi.

# 2

## Psalms
## of Creation

I wake up and a new day has begun. There is air to breathe…daylight. The earth
is renewing itself with sunshine; or watering grass, gardens, and vegetations
with rain. Birds sing; waves lap upon the shore. The earth pulsates with life.
There is color, shade, sound, fragrance in the air, texture, temperature, a range
of tactile experiences to sample: from a pile of leaves to play in, grass to roll
on, or water at a nearby pool or beach to dive into.

Most of us have a place we like to go that we call sanctuary; a place that is
restful, healing, beautiful, and revitalizing. I have a number of these places.
One is close by, requiring only that I step outside my front door. There I can
view the waters of English Bay, walk along the seawall, listen to the waves crash
along the shore, hear seabirds, and smell the salt in the air. I can walk over to
the park, where a colony of great blue herons has over 35 nests. The herons
are unexpected. In decline in most of my home province of British Columbia,
this colony has made a rebound adjacent to metropolitan Vancouver.[1] I take
care to notice everything around me and of all the creatures that have found a
home nearby, I am learning to live as neighbor to the great blue heron. Other
neighbors complain about the noise they make, the squawking sounds when
they copulate. The baby herons rise at dawn, flying around the trees in the park
and over my apartment building. I often hear them if I am sleeping lightly. For
me, their sound is joyful. It resonates with the gleefulness any infant, regardless
of species, makes when it is learning to do something new.

I try to walk near my home daily. I have a route that usually includes Vancouver's Lost Lagoon. On my way, I encounter raccoons, squirrels, chipmunks, skunk, occasionally a coyote or beaver, swans, geese, and other waterfowl. I walk past giant Douglas fir, spruce, and hemlock trees; past fern groves, lily pads, hollyhocks, and rhododendron bushes. With each walk, I rub shoulders with these different beings.

While some people begin their day with the news, I begin it with a fresh encounter with the natural environment outside my home. Over time, I become acquainted with the cycles of the year and the activities of birds nesting, squirrels gathering nuts, flowers and trees changing color, the temperatures of the season shifting. I count to see if all eight swans are in the lagoon. I notice the colors of the sky and vegetation reflected in the water. I take in the sounds of birds, wind in the trees, a dog coming ashore and shaking off the water while holding a stick in its mouth.

The constant feeling that accompanies my daily walk is one of enjoyment. In every direction, I encounter the generosity of creation. A sunrise, a leaf turning yellow, geese landing on the water, the scent of a rose garden. I notice that the simple act of putting on my shoes and going outside refreshes and renews me, even when it is raining.

Being born in Vancouver, I got used to rain early on – tasting it with my tongue, getting wet in my yellow rain jacket but staying dry underneath, listening to the sound of rain in the forest as I stood beneath an old-growth cedar tree. From the snows of winter, the blooming flower gardens in the spring, the summer berries, and the changing fall colors, I learned of the benevolence of creation. I learned that every day offered novelty, as both subtle and dramatic changes in the environment invited me to be curious about the land in which I was living.

When the psalms speak of creation, they express gratitude. The experience of having air to breathe, water to drink, warmth from the sun, the earth to walk upon with all its splendors – these are all given to us when we are born. We receive these gifts of life, not as a result of dislocation or upheaval, but as part of our daily existence. Our stewardship of the earth affects the quality of the air we breathe and the water we drink. Yet the focus of these psalms is one of celebration for what God has created here on earth. Our failure to be good stewards of the earth is part of what we can lament – a type of psalm addressed in a future chapter.

Walter Brueggemann writes of the response to the reliability and generosity of God's creation found in the creation psalms.

> The community that composes and sings these psalms readily affirmed that this experience is ordained and sustained by God. A proper response is one of gratitude.
>
> The world is God's way of bestowing blessing upon us. Our times are ordered by God according to the seasons of life, according to the needs of the day. In all these processes, we find ourselves to be safe and free...[2]

Gratitude and the desire to express it is something that can come almost unbidden when we simply make a space to notice what is around us. At a recent poetry workshop, with the Canadian poet Patrick Lane, participants were asked to write a poem in praise of the sacred in the ordinary. As I pondered my homework, I returned to the room in which I was staying at the retreat center on the southern edge of Vancouver Island, where the workshop was being hosted. I thought nothing could be more ordinary than my guestroom, which I had judged to be unremarkable. Yet in that room, a poem emerged as I simply looked around at what was present within the room and visible outside the window. I titled my poem, *A Poem about a Story, and Other Things I Found in My Guestroom at Sooke, BC.*

> I'm trying to find inspiration in this cold little room,
> a guest for three nights in this ocean-side lodging.
> Back propped against the wall,
> I'm giving thanks for these simple things:
>> carpet beneath me,
>> wool jacket around me,
>> bare light bulb above me,
>> and a night table beside me.

I'm having a little glass of wine.

Across the room I see the wall hanging:
a small wooden frame containing a print
depicting an ancient Celtic tale,
– three women who created the Earth.

I praise the maiden Africa,
who gave birth to earth to the beat of a drum,
who sent a crow across the universe to announce its arrival,
who listened for a name, ancient as star or dirt, to give to it,
who poured libations, breathed on it, tattooed and shaped earth
into oceans, continents.

I praise the mother India,
who washed the earth in the Ganges River,
who took it for an elephant ride,
who charmed earth with a snake, protected it with a mongoose,
who rocked it to sleep.

I praise the old native crone,
who saw earth emerge from the sea on a turtle's back,
who blessed earth with sweet grass,
who wiped earth's brow,
who told earth stories of brother sun and sister moon.

My glass is empty.

I look through the window,
across the meadow,
past old apple trees, to the sea;
give thanks for the earth,
this ancient guestroom.

When any one of us seeks to give thanks for creation, if we allow for creativity to take hold, we do not know what will emerge. Often, a poem simply writes itself. A song is given voice. A psalm is born. Writing this poem on that chilly February night at the retreat center, I remembered creation stories I had heard at storytellers' festivals. The print in the wooden frame served as a prompt to recall these stories. Because creation is constantly introducing novelty, we find ourselves in new surroundings or encountering old surroundings in new circumstances as our lives change. As stillness in the presence of creation takes hold, we can begin to access emotions and ideas that we did not know were lying ready to spring forth. When faced with the beauty and wonder of creation, words *do* come, expressing our thankfulness and praise.

Zen-poet Norman Fischer's version of Psalm 33 conveys amazement at what the Holy One has done.

> Uprightness and justice are the shape of your love...
> The heavens are made of your word
> and animated by your breath...
> The earth is awestruck
> and all that lives stands openmouthed.
> For in your speaking the unsayable word
> all that is comes to be.
> Your saying bursts forth
> and all holds fast.[3]

The impact of what the Creator is doing in creation leaves the earth awestruck; all living beings stand open-mouthed. In this psalm, we encounter the challenge of describing the wonder of creation and the hand of the Creator, which often leave us speechless.

The lure to celebrate what the Holy has done in creation is heard from voices across religions and centuries. This sense of awe at what is created is found in the psalm-like *Du'a* said on the 27th day of Ramadan.

> O Lord of the clear heavens and the light and darkness in them:
> O Lord of the outspread lands and the creatures and created
> things in them:
> O Lord of the steadfast mountains:
> O Lord of the sweeping winds...[4]

In this prayer said during this sacred holy month in the Muslim religious calendar, followers repeat a long list of manifestations of what the Lord has done in creation.

In the Aztec poem known as the Madrid Codex, the coming of the dawn is celebrated as a sign of new life.

> Awaken, already the sky is tinged with red,
> already the dawn has come,
> already the flame-colored pheasants are singing,
> the fire-colored swallows,
> already butterflies are on the wing.[5]

While only fragments of the Madrid Codex survived the Spanish conquest of Mexico, the vividness of the description of dawn's arrival suggests a people who, like us, also experienced awe at creation.

Many sacred Hindu writings are expressed in prose, but some of the writings of Hindu poets resemble the ponderings of the Hebrew psalmists. Here is one from the poet Tulsidas (1532–1623), who became famous as the "composer of the *Ramacaritamanasa*...which has become 'the Bible of Northern India.'"[6]

> Looking at your extremely varied creation
> the mind that tries to understand it reels.[7]

The testimony of sacred literature across the ages shows a common impulse to praise the Creator for the works of creation.

In the Hebrew Psalms, we find the poet paying attention to what is occurring in creation. This is key for anyone wanting to write a new psalm. Taking time to notice both the grand and the miniscule in creation brings us closer to the work of the Creator. This can inspire us to give praise for the creation. In Psalm 104, the writer portrays the earth as God's dwelling place.

> Only you stretch out the curtain of the sky,
>     lay the beams of your palace in the oceans
>
> — PSALM 104:2B–3A

Further along in the psalm, God is praised for the orderliness of creation. The waters that once covered all the earth have been given boundaries (verses 6–9), rain falls (verse 13), harvests are bountiful (verses 13–14), bread is made (verse 15), wine is enjoyed (verse 16), trees provide nests for birds (verse 17), and hills and boulders are habitat for mountain goats and rock badgers (verse 18) The splendor of God's ordering of creation is found in daily signs of the Creator's design.

> You have made the moon to mark the seasons;
>     the sun knows its time for setting.
> You make darkness and it is night...
> When the sun rises...
>     People go out to their work
>     and to their labor until the evening.
>
> — PSALM 104:19–20, 22–23 (NRSV)

Within the orderliness of the earth, allowance is given for the upheaval of earthquakes and eruptions of volcanoes.

> When God looks at the world, it quakes;
>     at a touch, the mountains smoke.
>
> — PSALM 104:32

This is the domain of a God who is "clothed in majesty and splendor and wrapped in a robe of light" (verse 1b–2a). In response, the psalmist vows to sing psalms to God throughout all of life and, in verse 34, prays that "my meditation please the Lord, as I show my joy" in God.

### *Exercise:* **In Praise of Creation**

With a notebook or journal and your favorite writing implement, go to a place where you are in the presence of creation. It may be a park, a beach, a riverbank, a meadow, a hillside, a forest trail, a lake, your backyard, or outside your own front door. This is a place where you can encounter the beauty and wonder of creation. (If you wish, you can travel in your mind to a beautiful place you've visited that holds special appeal for you.) Take time to be still in this place of beauty. Sit or walk silently, observing this natural setting. As you attune yourself to the expression of creation around you, begin to write down what you notice, describing the following.

What lives here? (animals, birds, fish, vegetation...)

I see...

I hear...

I feel the texture of...

I smell...

How is the Creator present in this place? How is the Creator made known to you here?

What does this place remind you of?

Creation feels like...

Words I would use to describe creation include...

I want to tell the Creator that creation is, for me,...

When I consider creation, I would like to ask the Creator...

Viewing the whole of Creation, I am aware of the contrast of…

When I consider creation, I want to say the following phrase over and over again…

Something that I think others find amazing or awesome about creation is…

Because of creation, humans and other life forms on this planet can enjoy the following things…

Review what you have written, circling any words or phrases that interest you. In the previous chapter, various poetic devices found in the Hebrew Psalms were discussed. Note if any of these could be useful to you as you get ready to write a new psalm to creation.

- restatement
- lists
- citation
- statement and question
- questions
- contrast and reversal
- mixing of singular and plural
- the repetition of a word or a phrase
- an echo, expansion, or definition of a thought, emotion, or image
- acrostic poem
- simile or metaphor

Recalling these poetic devices, your own style of writing and your reflections on this encounter with a favorite place in nature, take time to make a few more notes about what stands out for you, about the impact and effect creation has on you, and about the source of this creation and its unfolding.

Now take time to compose your own creation psalm.

## ENDNOTES

[1] "Great blue heron stages comeback in park," CBC, Vancouver, Canada, April 2, 2004, http://www.cbc.ca/stories/2004/04/02/sci-tech/herons040402

[2] Walter Brueggemann, *Spirituality of the Psalms* (Minneapolis, MN: Augsburg Fortress, 2002), 22.

[3] Norman Fischer, *Opening to You: Zen-Inspired Translations of the Psalms* (New York: Viking, 2002), 51.

[4] Constance E. Padwick, *Muslim Devotions* (Oxford, England: Oneworld Publications, 1996), 250.

[5] Miguel Leon-Portilla, *Pre-Columbian Literature of Mexico* (Norman, Oklahoma: University of Oklahoma, 1969), 62.

[6] Klaus K. Klostermaier, *Hindu Writings: A Short Introduction to Major Sources* (Oxford, England: Oneworld Publications, 2000), 54.

[7] Ibid.

# 3

## Psalms of Thanksgiving and Praise

### PSALMS OF THANKSGIVING

In 1990, I was invited to be part of an international consultation among youth serving organizations near Limuru, Kenya, an hour's drive outside of Nairobi. Over 90 people attended, representing every continent and organizations such as the YMCA, YWCA, the World Council of Churches, and other youth and student movements. In that context, I learned many things about the challenges people face around the world. I learned about the challenge of providing programs to a new generation, which, in many parts of the world, lives with the realities of war, poverty, illiteracy, disease, scarce educational resources, leadership deficits, and resistance to the voices of youth.

During my travels in Kenya, I met people running local youth programs. This included being invited to be a guest of the bishop of the Church of the Holy Spirit (East Africa). I packed my bags on a Wednesday and waited. Three days later, on "Africa time," I was met by two enthusiastic young men who came to pick me up in the bishop's jeep.

The trip in the jeep covered about 200 miles and took nearly 12 hours. En route, a fan belt in the car engine broke and one of the guides had to hitchhike back to Nairobi to get it replaced. This caused us to be very late. As we traveled northwest of Nakuru, night fell. On a side road, we were stopped for over half an hour in an uncomfortable encounter with the Kenyan militia. Pointing their guns at the jeep, they demanded money. A payment was agreed upon and we left the checkpoint a little shaken, but relieved to have passed through.

The side roads had huge potholes. From my rear window, I could see men and women walking along the roadside, balancing baskets of goods on their heads. Exotic birds sounded our arrival as we rumbled into the rural village where the bishop lived, some 20 miles east of Uganda.

Though it was nearly midnight when we arrived, a meal was prepared. My hosts from Africa ate *ugali,* a dish of meal with chicken and broth served in a soup bowl. As their guest, I was given a leg of roast chicken, cooked on a BBQ spit on the earth outside the house. I was also brought something else very special for my meal – a very large, boiled potato. The potato was just for me. No one else would be having one for dinner. Next morning, in the darkness before dawn, one of my hosts got up and lit the fire to make breakfast. Roosters began to crow in anticipation of the dawn's light.

In this East-African village, I learned again to be grateful. I learned that a simple boiled potato can be a symbol of hospitality, a special dish served to a guest who has come all the way from North America. I learned that, in many countries, making breakfast means getting up at 4 a.m. I learned that tow trucks are not plentiful or reliable in many nations. I learned that I could go cruising in my car at home, and, within the speed limits, travel unhindered by the authorities. Meanwhile, my hosts traveling at night would pay military officers "tips" for patrolling the highways. I learned that, in much of the world, running according to schedule is a luxury. I learned to be thankful for what I had at home.

I also felt a deep gratitude for my brief three-week exposure to rural life in west Kenya. Memories of the people I met, their exuberance and the integrity of their quest to make their villages and youth programs thrive, continue to humble me.

Mary Jo Leddy, writing about gratitude, makes the following comment.

> In a culture of money, we tend to have a ledger view of life. We add up the pluses and minuses and try to account for our lives. In the process, we miss the amazing fact that we even have a life to add up. We take being alive for granted and move into a cost-benefit

analysis. Lost in the process is the incalculable mystery of simply being alive. The liberation of gratitude begins when we stop taking life for granted.[1]

The ledger view that Mary Jo Leddy speaks of can be all pervasive. In the adult world of responsibility, we have monthly rent or mortgage payments to make. While we find work to meet our payments, for many people work itself is a grind. The drive to get ahead can produce a perverse competitiveness between employees and businesses. In the 1947 film version of Charles Dickens' classic story *A Christmas Carol,* Ebenezer Scrooge and his business partner Jacob Marley are ambitious entrepreneurs. When the company they are part of discovers that members of the company board have been embezzling company funds, they propose to buy 51 percent of the shares in order to save its reputation. As the ledger grows for Scrooge and Marley, any gratitude they may once have had for the work they do is replaced by the god of greed.

At the end of each day, I name to God five things for which I am thankful. Simply being alive is one of them. The mystery of my own life is a source of gratitude. Born three weeks premature, I spent the first six weeks of my life in an incubator. My adjustment to the world was tenuous in those first weeks after birth. At one point, I weighed a mere three pounds, 12 ounces. However, I had the care of doctors and nurses, and the love of my mother and father, who lost a lot of sleep taking care of me and who provided the support and nurture that allowed me to be a happy and healthy baby boy.

For each of us, there is the story of our arrival out of the birth canal. At our first cry, no matter the circumstances surrounding our parenting, there was support from the universe to feed, shelter, and clothe us. There was enough of a response from the world we were born into, to carry us through infancy, childhood, youth, and into adulthood. While everyone can recount the inevitable wounds received from human families, school systems, peer groups, and the workplace, we also have much to be thankful for.

What springs to mind for you when you look back on the nurture you have received, enabling you to make it through life this far?

Psalms of thanksgiving have a number of features common to most other psalms. They

- address God,
- praise God,
- mention where and how thanks is given to God,
- describe what God has done for individuals or for the community,
- contain a list of thanks, or of the recalled deeds of God,
- invite others to give God thanks, and
- offer a plea to God.

Within a psalm of thanksgiving, these elements may occur at random, rather than in sequence. In many psalms, the focus of the psalmist can stray to other religious moods. A psalm of lament may contain a section of thanksgiving or vice versa.

In Psalm 138, these elements are easy to identify. Verse 1a addresses God. Verse 1b praises God. Verse 2a tells how and where thanks to God is given. Verse 2b remembers what God has done. Verses 3, 6, and 7 recall more of what God has done. Verses 4 and 5 invite others to give God thanks. Finally, verse 8 contains a plea to God to "not forsake the work of your hands."

> I give you thanks, O God,
>      with my whole heart;
> before the gods I sing your praise;
> I bow down toward your holy temple
>      and give thanks to your name
>      for your steadfast love and your faithfulness;
>      for you have exalted your name
>      and your word above everything.
> On the day I called,
>      you answered me,
>      you increased my strength of soul.
> All the rulers of the earth shall praise you, O God,
>      for they have heard the words of your mouth.

They shall sing of the ways of God,
for great is the glory of God.
For though God is high,
God regards the lowly;
but the haughty God perceives from far away.
Though I walk in the midst of trouble,
you preserve me against the wrath of my enemies;
you stretch out your hand,
and your mighty hand delivers me.
God will fulfill God's purpose for me;
your steadfast love, O God, endures forever.
Do not forsake the work of your hands.

— Psalm 138:1–8 (NTP)

Speak this psalm aloud. Take a moment to notice two poetic phrases that appeal to you. Where do you encounter a sense of momentum, movement, or flow in this psalm? Being aware of what appeals to us in the psalms we read can give us clues to what might work for us as we craft our own psalms. Writing a new psalm is not a work of imitation. However, it does involve noticing what works, what inspires us.

In his *Spirituality of the Psalms*, Walter Brueggemann has noted that the psalms of thanksgiving are songs of new orientation. This means that the individual or community has passed through a time of lament, complaint, or trouble. God has heard their cry, forgiven or healed their ills, and so their response is to give thanks. "These psalms tell stories of *going into the trouble* and *coming out of the trouble.*"[2] In other words, these psalms are not written out of a context of innocence. Despite life's obstacles, the writer returns to a place of radical gratitude.

**Exercise:** Let's get ready to write a psalm of thanksgiving.

How would you like to name God in your psalm?

What praise or thanks can you offer to God?

Comment on where or how you have given, or wish to give, God thanks.

What comes to mind first when you think about what God has done for you, your community, your nation, or the earth?

List other things that would cause or inspire you to give God thanks.

Who would you want to invite to join you in giving thanks to God?

What plea or cry would you offer for God to hear?

What trouble or adversity is behind you now?

Review what you have written. If you have written a response to each question or statement above, you have a sound basis for writing a new psalm of thanksgiving. While psalms of thanksgiving usually include all of these elements, there is no magic formula or specific guideline for how much time you need to spend attending to any particular element.

## PSALMS OF PRAISE

A variant on the psalm of thanksgiving is the psalm of praise. In his writings on the Psalms, Thomas Merton, a contemplative Trappist monk, noted that praise has metamorphosed into a marketing tool used to promote products to consumers in an acquisitive culture. Being able to discern what is worthy of our praise and what is just hype for products is spiritually important. Claims that overstate the value of something can erode our clarity, fogging our sense of what it means to truly give praise. As a consequence, we may not know what words to use when seeking to praise God. We may even lose our sense of why we might seek to give God praise. Writing in 1956, Merton observes that,

Praise is cheap today. Everything is praised. Soap, beer, toothpaste, clothing, mouthwash, movie stars, and the latest gadgets which are supposed to make life more comfortable – everything is constantly being "praised." Praise is now so overdone that everybody is sick of it, and since everything is "praised" with the official hollow enthusiasm of the radio announcer, it turns out in the end that *nothing* is praised. Praise has become empty. No one wants to use it.[3]

Praise psalms are usually list psalms. The psalmist makes a list of places, people, things, occasions, and reasons to praise God.

> O praise God.
> Praise God in heaven;
>    praise God in the heights.
> Praise God, all God's angels.
>    Praise God, all God's host.
> Praise God, sun and moon;
>    praise God, all you shining stars;
> praise God, heaven of heavens,
> and you waters above the heavens.
>    Let them all praise the name of God,
>       for God spoke the word and they were created;
>    Fire and hail, snow and ice,
>       gales of wind obeying God's voice;
>    all mountains and hills;
>       all fruit-trees and all cedars;
>    wild beasts and cattle,
>       creeping things and winged birds
>
> – Psalm 148:1–5, 8–10 (NEB)

In Psalm 148, the poet uses the repetition of the phrase, praise God. Later in the psalm, the poet simply makes a list without the use of a repeated phrase.
Read Psalms 146, 147, 149, and 150 as other examples of praise psalms.

In his *Book of Mercy,* the poet Leonard Cohen offers readers 50 psalms. Among them can be found a psalm composed in the "praise psalm" style. Listing the things he believes are holy, Cohen creates a litany of praise to the One whose "name is praised forever."[4]

Simply by using words or phrases such as holy, praise, thanks, to You, marvelous, wondrous, blessing and honor, the poet creates an entry point to the many aspects of praise that are being offer to the almighty.

C. S. Lewis once remarked, "I think we delight to praise what we enjoy because the praise not merely expresses but completes the enjoyment; it is its appointed consummation."[5] In the psalms of praise, the psalmists invite us to include God in our natural inclination to compliment what is worthy of our regard and care.

*Exercise:* In your journal or notebook, make a list of people, places, creatures, and occasions that inspire you to give praise to God.

Review what you have written. You can choose to repeat a phrase such as "praise God," or make a long list, without punctuating the invitation to praise. Using what you know about the different devices used in psalm writing, write a new psalm of praise.

## ENDNOTES

[1] Mary Jo Leddy, *Radical Gratitude* (New York: Orbis Books, 2003), 40.

[2] Walter Brueggemann, *Spirituality of the Psalms* (Minneapolis, MN: Augsburg Fortress, 2002), 50.

[3] Thomas Merton, *Praying the Psalms* (Collegeville, Minnesota: The Liturgical Press, 1956), 10.

[4] Leonard Cohen, *Book of Mercy* (Toronto: McClelland & Stewart, 1984), number 43.

[5] C. S. Lewis, *Reflections on the Psalms* (London: Geoffrey Bles, 1958), 95.

# 4

## *Psalms of Lament*

Lamentation as a social practice in the 21st century is most closely associated with the erection of walls used for ritual grief. Along Israel's Western (retaining) Wall, there is a place where members of the Jewish community gather to wail. Each Friday they gather to mourn their fallen state. Some cry loudly in anguish. Others press their lips against crevices in the masonry. It is as if they anticipate an answer from within the wall. Since the Six-Day War and the enhanced status of the state of Israel, many regard the wall as a place of celebration.

The Holocaust Memorial in Miami, Florida, has a wall with the names of people who died in the concentration camps during the Second World War. The memorial also contains a giant sculpture of an outstretched arm and hand reaching into the sky.[1] The arm itself is covered with smaller sculptures of tormented people in family groupings. Sculptor Kenneth Treister says, "This is my portrayal of the Holocaust... A giant outstretched arm, tattooed with a number from Auschwitz, rises from the earth, the last reach of a dying person. Each visitor has his own interpretation...some see despair... some hope...some the last grasp for life...and for some it asks a question to God... "Why?"

The Veterans Memorial in Washington, DC, lists the names of all the soldiers who died in Vietnam. A large number of AIDS memorials, including one in Vancouver, Canada, list the names of people who have died of this disease.

The reasons for lament are many: our grief over our inner state, the cruelty of humanity during wartime, the ravages of disease. Faced with our mortality and our choices – individual and collective – we lament. Without places to ritually express our grief, something essential in our humanness gets shut off.

In the foreword to Ann Weems' book *Psalms of Lament,* Walter Brueggemann observes that "What strikes one about the book of Psalms, if one notices anything at all, is that nearly one half of the Psalms are songs of lament and poems of complaint."[2]

The psalms of lament are usually identified as a lament for an individual's troubles, or a lament for a community. These psalms speak powerfully of humanity's suffering, and of the struggle to bring this experience before God. They also usually include an expression of trust or thanksgiving, despite the devastation or turmoil that has occurred.

In Psalm 77, notice the detailed description of the condition of the psalmist, who is in deep distress.

> In my day of distress I sought the Holy One,
>     stretching out my hands all night long –
>     yet I was not comforted.
> I think of God, and groan;
>     I ponder, and my spirit faints.
> You prevent my eyes from closing;
>     I am too upset to talk.
> I think of days long ago,
>     of years long past.
> At night I remember my songs;
>     I examine my heart,
>     and question my spirit.
> "O Holy One, will you reject us forever
>     and never again show us favor?
> Has your faithful love ceased to exist?
>     Has your promise failed for all generations?
> Have you forgotten how to be gracious?
>     Have you in anger shut off your compassion forever?"

I said, "This is my sorrow:
  The hand of the Most High has lost its power."

– PSALM 77:2–10

In this psalm, we encounter the poet's use of emotion. We know how this writer feels: troubled, discomforted, moaning, faint, speechless. God's action seems puzzling: "You prevent my eyes from closing." The poet lists a series of questions asked of God. It is only later in this psalm that the poet can be comforted by bringing to mind God's deeds: "Then I remember your works, the wonderful things you did of old. I meditate on all you have done and ponder your activities" (verse 11).

Writing a psalm of lament can be demanding as it invites us to face our grief and suffering. Writing such a psalm requires that we stop and pay attention to the places deep in our hearts that can be obscured by distraction, busyness, avoidance, and denial. At a time in my life when I had finished a very rewarding yet demanding job, I experienced deep fatigue. My recovery took longer than I could ever have imagined. I was so used to being active. Here is a psalm I wrote during that time in my life.

Is this what you want me to do God? Sleep? For four months?
  Haven't I waited before you?
Haven't I sought you, my refuge and my strength?
  What trick is this, to give me exhaustion as a daily companion?
Even in my sleep I am not refreshed.
  I wake each morning, fatigued.
I try to think of a word; it escapes me.
  I walk to get something;
  arriving, I do not know my purpose.
Must memory and concentration be depleted?
  I look at people who I have known a long time;
  I can't remember their names.
This is not living!
  You can do better God.
You are the God who made me;

You are not finished with me
and I am not finished with you.
Repair me,
help me live again.
Around me I see the work of your creation.
You give birds a song to sing, rising early at dawn.
You give breath to the runner,
an idea to the teacher.
How wonderfully made are the works of your creation,
You, who carve us in the palm of your hand.
Rouse yourself God. While I lie on my bed, napping,
the tongues of the gossip find new vigor.
Remember your dream for me,
and I will follow your path.
Because You have heard me,
I know you will restore my vitality.
I will walk and not grow weary;
I will run and not grow faint.

Taking time to acknowledge what was happening to me was an essential part of moving forward. Bringing myself before God during that confusing and disorienting episode of fatigue, helped to express my lament. Once I felt my lament deep within, my vision for returned strength was even clearer, and I wanted God to help me with this.

What places in your heart have spoken to you of lament? What feelings have you experienced in the face of betrayal; failure; loss; death; sickness; family difficulties; money problems; conflict; broken relationship; isolation; work and employment problems; injustice and violence between peoples and nations, and with the earth and all the species that inhabit it?

Walter Brueggemann identifies six elements within the psalms of lament. These elements are

- an intimate address or naming of God,
- a complaint, which is brought before God,
- a petition for God to act,

- a motivation, which is added to bolster the petition so that God will act,
- a request to punish the adversary, usually expressed in deep anguish or distress, and
- an expression of "confidence, well-being, and gratitude" in being heard by God.[3]

That the lament psalms end with an expression of confidence, well-being, and gratitude is evidence that they were cathartic for the psalmist. The psalm does not end on the same note on which it began. Something has shifted within the writer. Through the act of describing the trouble and suffering, something has been healed, or put at ease.

In her book *Psalms of Lament,* Ann Weems shares 50 psalms that explore the devastation she experienced as a result of the death of her son. By expressing her grief and rage through psalm writing, she discovered a powerful vehicle that allowed her to begin to come to terms with her Creator and the loss she suffered.

I recently came face to face with my own lament upon hearing an address by Stephen Lewis, Canada's ambassador to the United Nations responsible for responding to the HIV/AIDS crisis in Africa. Fresh from recent visits to that continent, his stories of heartbreak and hope stirred me. I was awakened to the bell-like clarity of his call to move beyond complacency, inertia, triviality, and contentment. Two stories from northern Uganda stayed with me for days after his speech. The first described the desperation in the Gulu district and the ravages of over a decade of military conflict and the dislocation of nearly two million people. The second story was one of hope. In the rural community of Arua in northwest Uganda, people have moved beyond the shame and stigma of AIDS and have begun to invite people living with AIDS to teach the wider community how to stay safe and to not be afraid of those who have the virus.[3] Reflecting on these stories, I wrote the following lament.

Have you not heard the news, Holy One?
   Have you not seen?
Word has come from Northern Uganda.
   from the district of Gulu.

Daily children are abducted, abused, murdered
   by the Lord's Resistance Army.
Do you not hear the cries where nine out of ten people
   live in camps, displaced from their homes?
Nearly two million people live here, God,
   fear is everywhere.
At a camp at Pagak, thirty-one are killed,
   five hundred huts
   burnt to the ground.
Untidy mounds of earth and rock
   mark graves of one more slaughter.
Children are not safe, and each night
   forty thousand walk several miles
   to makeshift shelters of safety in Gulu town.
Little children of four, five, six, seven and eight,
   straggle in single file at dusk along road's edge,
   ghost-like, emerging from darkness.
Family life is dismembered
   soldiers rape women and young girls.
Who can stop them?
   AIDS overwhelms families and health workers
   and where is the money to buy drugs?
God, enough of this devastation.
   Women are dying.
   Children as young as six are the heads of their households.
It's not right, God.
   It's not right.
Where have you been, Holy One
   and what is your plan?
And yet, you have remembered the village people of Arua.
   You have not forgotten the north-west.
Even now, eleven hundred receive medication;
   people living with AIDS are welcomed.

People tell stories, grow in wisdom and remain healthy;
    the stigma evaporates.
Your compassion is bestowed
    and people see each other with new eyes.
May your guiding hand stretch out to all who need you.
    May you come quickly
and shelter all who cry out with Your care.

As you read this psalm, what do you notice first? What word or phrase jumps off the page for you? What emotions are evoked in you? What are some of the elements that make this a psalm of lament?

In writing any new psalm, the individual will make choices about which literary elements to include from the mix available. As noted above, there can be quite a variety of emphases within any given psalm, so it is important to be open to both the spirit that is present to you, and the literary forms or devices you would like to use as you compose your psalm. With psalms of lament, the emotion may be raw. Use the structure of the psalm to give shape to your words. Also allow the spirit to guide you, so that you do not turn your psalm into a checklist of elements and leave out the wildness of your lament.

### *Exercise:* Expressing Your Lament

Think of your own life circumstances, the sources of disquiet, distress, or despair. Complete the following sentence stems.

I am troubled by...

It has been painful for me to express...

When I try to avoid... I...

I lament...

When I consider the suffering of...

In my silence, I cry for...

I want God to know...

If only God would...

If I could only show or remind God... then God would...then I would be grateful to God at last for...

Re-read what you have written. Now take some time to write your psalm of lament to God.

### Endnotes

[1] See photo at http://www.holocaustmmb.org

[2] Ann Weems, *Psalms of Lament* (Louisville: Westminster John Knox Press, 1995), 22.

[3] Ibid., xi–xiii.

[4] For background on these and other stories and how you can help, visit www.stephenlewisfoundation.org

# 5

## *Psalms of Confession*

In his book *Opening Up. The Healing Power of Expressing Emotions,* Dr. James Pennebaker explores the dynamics of self-disclosure. He wonders what determines the optimal circumstances for confiding something.[1]

Working with other therapists and medical researchers, Pennebaker conducted a number of studies designed to measure the benefits to health, psyche, and spirit that might arise from confession. He concluded that simply talking or writing about an event produced minimal benefits. (People who *never* wrote about or discussed their troubles were the least healthy members of society.) *Thinking* about personal problems, without doing anything else, proved even less effective and only served to prolong or increase mental and emotional suffering and misery. Although thinking about something we feel guilt or shame for, or cannot forgive ourselves for, can bring the situation to our awareness, like a skipping record, we only get so far, repeating a line of thought in our head until we fall exhausted from overanalyzing. Punishing inner voices and stuck emotional patterns hold sway, pinning us to a wall of endless self-recrimination, or sending us down a well of inner turmoil.

If we decide to move towards confession, our heart and mind must listen to each other; we must bring to the conversation the rigor of the mind and the honesty of the heart. Without the mind, we may kid ourselves about what's at stake in the situation we wish to confess, thereby failing to learn from our experience. Without the heart, we may not be able to access the worlds of compassion and forgiveness, which are important spiritual benefits of confession.

Pennebaker's studies showed that the health benefits of confession correlate to the degree of seriousness of the personal experience. They also relate to the degree the person expresses their emotions, compared with past patterns of inhibition.[2] Confession can be an especially fruitful way to deal with some of the most difficult experiences in human relationships: war, abuse, torture, betrayal, deception, cheating (like on an exam), stealing, slander, gossip, dishonesty, despair, anger, confusion, discrimination, bankruptcy, faithlessness in a significant relationship, perfectionism, pride, envy, greed, and vanity.

When we confess something that has been weighing on us, it becomes possible to realign our heart and our mind. Forgiveness of self and other is again possible. Compassion can be reignited. Without confession, our attempts at forgiveness and compassion can be muted and strained, a sign that something within us is blocked and needs our attention.

Two obstacles to confession are the vulnerability of shame and the power of shamelessness. For the person who often feels ashamed, there is a danger that they may use the exercise of confession to undermine their ability to love and be loved. In the 1995 British movie *Little Voice,* Jane Horrocks plays a woman named Laura, who lives with her mother above a record store that her late father ran. Her mother nicknames her "Little Voice," because she is quiet and shy; she rarely speaks and hardly ever leaves her tiny attic room. Sometimes, it seems as if sorry is the only word Laura knows. Laura spends her time listening to her father's vast record collection and talking to his ghost. She has cultivated an ability to mimic many great vocalists, including Marilyn Monroe and Shirley Bassey. Her mother's boyfriend, played by Michael Caine, is a failed talent agent. He sees a way to make a killing from Laura's voice and plots to get her to perform in public.

Laura's widowed mother, Mari, played by Brenda Blethyn, is a middle-aged woman who lives life to its fullest. Unfortunately, Mari is also unkind, vain, vapid, shameless, and motivated solely by self-interest. Her two main interests are drinking and sex. Mari finds it difficult to imagine that she has ever done anything wrong. She seems to suffer no doubt. Yet she is always eager to identify the latest fault of her nearly speechless daughter. Beneath her bluster, Mari is miserable and intellectually and emotionally feeble.

Confession will look very different for the Lauras of the world than it will for persons like her mother, Mari.

Here is a confession that Laura might bring before God.

> Dear God,
>     I confess that I find it hard to stand up for myself.
> My mother tells me that I am useless; I just let her say it.
>     I tell myself it doesn't matter.
> Many times when I am yelled at, I tell myself it doesn't matter.
> Sometimes I think that *I* don't matter.
>
>     God, I confess I have tried to convince myself of a lie.
> It *docs* matter. I don't deserve to be treated this way.
>     You are probably wondering, God, if I matter to myself.
> But deep inside, God, I do believe that I matter.
>     Help me remember that I matter to you.
> Help me respect myself.
>     Help me to ask for what I need
>     so that I can ask others to remember to treat me with care.
> Laura

Living with shame, year after year, can cripple a person's spirit. The drive to withdraw from others, as Laura does in *Little Voice,* can be incredibly strong. The opportunity that confession can bring for someone such as Laura, to re-unite heart and mind, and to embrace a new attitude that is more life-giving, can be very healing.

For a person who has been bound by the cords of shame, it is important to remember that confession is not supposed to be an exercise in reigniting its punishing messages. Take time to notice any self-sabotaging actions before launching into a ritual, or before talking, or writing a prayer or psalm of confession. Confession is a step towards freedom from the things that hold us back from living a more abundant life.

While Laura's mother, Mari, is not a likely person to ever write a psalm of confession, it is possible to imagine what her inner life is like, because there are enough telltale signs in the movie. Her character is quite well-developed so that many sides of her personality are on display.

Here is a psalm of confession that Mari might write or speak as she becomes more honest with her heart and mind, and about the truth of her life.

Dear God,
Everyone says I'm the life of the party.
  They count on me to eat, drink, dance, smoke, wisecrack,
  gossip.
O God, who am I fooling?
  I tell myself that everything I do is wonderful, fabulous,
  sensational.
But look at me.
  I'm all bluster and no substance.
When I'm honest with myself, my life feels so superficial,
so trivial.
I just don't get it, God:
  Why am I so unhappy when I am spending so much time
  doing the things I want to do?
There's an angry edge to me, God. I throw tantrums.
  What is becoming of me?
And my daughter:
  Why am I such a bully to her?
Why do I say such rude and offensive things to her?
  Why do I try to get a kick out of being
  hurtful and cruel to those I say I love?
And why am I so gullible?
  God, you saw my desperation in a grandiose plan
  to make money from my daughter's voice
  by launching a singing career she never asked for.
Now I feel anxious and depressed.
O God, save me from deluding myself.
  Help me to give myself a good hard look in the mirror.
Help me to listen to my daughter, Laura.

Help me to listen to you, too, God,
and to find my way back to you.
Mari

The script for the movie *Little Voice* never included these prayers of confession. Yet what a difference it might make for the shamed and the shameless to confess to God. It would mean they would have to be honest about what their lives consist of. Obstacles to living a more loving and freeing life could be examined. New growth could occur.

For those of us who are burdened by shame, or who are oblivious to the hurt and harm we cause by our intimidation and confrontation with the world around us, confession may be a way to restore balance to our inner lives and to our relationships with those with whom we live and work.

The psalm of confession often contains features similar to other psalms in the Hebrew psalter.

- The writer addresses God.
- The writer asks God to hear a confession.
- The writer shares with God their insight into the problem, and their part in it.
- The writer pleads with God, sometimes adding an incentive or motive, to hear and respond.

Can you spot these elements in Psalm 51?

Have mercy on me, O God, in your faithful love;
wipe clean the record of my wrongdoing.
Wash away the stains of disobedience;
cleanse me from my awful guilt.
I know too well the wrongs I've done,
haunted always by my guilt.
Against you, you alone have I sinned;
what is evil in your eyes, that I have done.
Your verdict against me is just,
your judgment what I fully deserve...

Create in me a clean heart;
    give me a new and steadfast spirit.
Cast me not away from your presence;
    take not your holy spirit from me.
Restore to me the joy of your saving help;
    by your bountiful spirit sustain me.
Let me teach your ways to the wicked,
    then sinners will return to you.

            – Psalm 51:1–4, 10–13

The language of confession can feel desperate. How often do we confess our sin? This is not comfortable language and speaking about our feelings of regret, shame, guilt, helplessness, powerlessness, despair, or rage can feel very foreign to our usual way of talking about our lives. What words would you use to describe how you feel when you sense you have missed the mark?

Being able to write a confession means being aware of who you are and the way your choices impact on your own life and the lives of others. In her book *Awakening Intuition,* Mona Lisa Shultz writes about "the conflict of autonomy versus shame and doubt, or initiative versus guilt."[3] Exploring what drives people toward or away from the opportunities in front of them, Shultz suggests that each person has drives for power, vulnerability, and relationship. The patterns that emerge over time with each choice we make tend to reinforce a particular behavior, causing us to repeat a movement toward or away from what is available to us. Below are pairings of words or phrases based on her observations of different preferences in the use of power, vulnerability, and the way we approach relationships.[4] By noticing our preferred way of being in the world, the way we act when faced with choices at work or at home, we can learn more about what drives us. Changing any pattern in our life requires attention. However, if we can believe the psalmists, with God all things are possible.

*Exercise:* Look at the following pairs of words and phrases. Circle the word or phrase within each A/B pairing that describes you best. Don't take a lot of time to decide; just make a gut choice.

Being honest with myself about the way I am in the world, I would describe myself as:

| | |
|---|---|
| A) mistrustful | B) trusting |
| A) standing alone | B) belonging |
| A) active | B) passive |
| A) uninhibited | B) fearful |
| A) direct | B) indirect |
| A) I always take the initiative | B) I wait for things to come |
| A) shameless | B) shameful |
| A) I am independent | B) I am dependent |
| A) I am needed by others | B) I need others |
| A) I take whatever I can get | B) I am a very giving person |
| A) I have well defined boundaries | B) I have very poor boundaries |
| A) I oppose others | B) I cooperate with others |
| A) I tell myself I am resilient | B) I tell myself I can't cope |
| A) I create my life | B) things happen the way they should |
| A) competitive | B) non-competitive |
| A) strive to win over others | B) compromise and make concessions |
| A) joy and exuberance | B) serenity and peace |
| A) isolation | B) intimacy |
| A) martyrdom | B) nurturance |
| A) passion | B) love |
| A) expression | B) comprehension |
| A) speaking | B) listening |
| A) linear | B) non-linear |
| A) law-abiding | B) risk-taking |
| A) a clear sense of purpose in life | B) an undefined purpose in life |

When I review the descriptive words or phrases I circled, I notice...

When I think about the person I am, the other things I know about myself are...

Some of the things I value as being beneficial and celebrate about the way I move and act in the world are...

Some of the things I do, or forget to do, that keep me from being at my best – with myself or with others – are...

I find it hard to forgive myself for...

I find it hard to forgive others for...

I want to confess before God...

I want to ask God...

I want to tell God that I am aware of...

Take time to review everything you have written. Choose a quiet moment to write a psalm of confession, addressing it to God, identifying what you wish to confess, sharing insights or observations you have about this situation, and offering a plea to the holy.

### ENDNOTES

[1] James Pennebaker, *Opening Up: The Healing Power of Expressing Emotions* (New York: The Guilford Press, 1997), 169–179.

[2] Kathleen Adams, *Write Way to Wellness* (Lakewood, Colorado: The Center for Journal Therapy), 3.

[3] Mona Lisa Shultz, *Awakening Intuition* (New York: Three Rivers Press, 1998), 168.

[4] Ibid., 141, 169, 199, 218, 249, 275.

# 6

## Psalms of Trust and Confidence

In his book *Healing and the Mind,* Bill Moyers interviews Rachel Naomi Remen, co-founder of Commonweal Cancer Help Program, and Clinical Professor of Family and Community Medicine at the University of California, San Francisco. In discussing her work with cancer patients, Remen comments on the relationship patients have with each other and with their doctors once the diagnosis of cancer has been reached:

> All people are wounded, but the people who come here can't cover it up the way the rest of us do... Everybody has pain, everybody is wounded. And because the participants can't cover up their woundedness, now that they have cancer, they can trust each other. You see, it's our woundedness that allows us to trust each other. I can trust another person only if I can sense that they, too, have woundedness, have pain, have fear. Out of that trust we can begin to pay attention to our own wounds and to each other's wounds – and to heal and be healed.[1]

If this is true in the relationship between cancer patients, and between patient and doctor, is this also true of the relationship we have with the Holy One? Do we relate to a God who knows no pain or fear? A God who has suffered no wounds? Or does the Creator know firsthand the experience of suffering? Does that experience serve in some way to motivate God to move toward us in our time of deepest need? And in our experience of God's care in the midst of our suffering, do we then grow in our trust and confidence that God will be present to us?

From the many images of the Divine portrayed within the Hebrew and Christian scriptures, it is clear that God will be who God will be. The face of the God we come to know changes, or is different, depending on our circumstances. But the one constant is that God is present whatever our circumstance. The psalmist writes, "If I climb up to heaven, you are there, if I make my bed in Sheol, again I find you." In the Qur'an there are 99 names for the Almighty. In Psalm 77, the poet wonders if "God's arm hangs powerless."

For many Christians, the crucifix – the cross with Jesus nailed upon it – is an incredibly powerful symbol. Jesus is called the Son of God. Part of the mysterious Trinity, this aspect of God's self suffers mightily.

Whatever our spiritual background and practices may be, the relationship between trust and suffering, and the impact this has on our relationship with God deserves our attention. For some people, the idea that God would feel pain, know fear, or suffer is deeply troubling. For others, the suggestion that God would *not* have firsthand experience of these feelings is equally astounding. It remains for each one of us in our walk with God to uncover what the sources of our trust in God may be. Our answer will have an impact on how we make meaning as we encounter the inevitable storms of life.

As we move through daily life, the opportunities to trust that God is with us abound. One day I can be serving a hot meal of beef stew to 200 homeless people on the downtown eastside of Vancouver. The next day I am learning to travel down white water rapids on the Nahatlatch River in British Columbia, or on the Nehanee River in Alaska. In both of these situations, a "river of trust" must be crossed. In serving the meal, there is the crush of people hungry from being on the streets and the demands for second helpings. The integrity of spirit these people show is mixed with the ravages of poverty due to chronic unemployment, drug addiction, or mental illness. On the rafting trip, there are the physical challenges of cold water, waves, unpredictable current, and raft mates I haven't met before. In both cases, I have a choice to trust that I am in the right place and that the Holy One has guided me there.

A choice *not* to trust but to worry could focus my attention on such questions as "What if we run out of food? What if someone is hard to deal with?" or "What if we drown? What if I don't have any fun?" We need to consciously take a stance of trust. To bring forth an intention to trust in God as we face our various challenges – service, adventure, learning, working – makes a difference in how we live each day.

Too often in our North American culture, our stance is one of control and fear. We live behind gated communities. We drive our children to school, fearful of predators. We don't take off our shoes to walk in the park, fearful of stepping on broken glass or garbage. It is true that we live in a world inhabited by thieves, child molesters, and litterbugs and that we need to take practical precautions. But should we focus on these negative things, or on our trust in God? For many, the overriding fear of danger and the need to be in control can leave us tense, anxious, and hesitant. In my province, 15 percent of high school students take antidepressants or other drugs to deal with the stress of life. Is this necessary?

As a society, we need to stop and ask ourselves what our fear and our need for control cost us in terms of our relationship with ourselves, our neighbors, and our God. Trusting too heavily in technology and science despite its many innovations and contributions to modern life can set us up for a fall. The NASA space program, to name only one example, has seen its share of disasters as well as many successes. The reality that we are fallible and fragile is a hard truth to swallow.

The stock market and real estate market can produce big winners in the chase to acquire greater financial stability. Yet trusting in these markets has also yielded multiple stories of financial ruin.

Trusting in military weaponry can become an obsession, as nations seek to defend themselves against unknown threats. The administration of George W. Bush spent its first eight months in office promoting the creation of a half-trillion dollar Ballistic Missile Defense System to shoot down incoming enemy missiles from "rogue nations." Yet the World Trade Center attacks on September 11, 2001, were achieved by terrorists who hijacked civilian planes using box cutters. Since the days of David and Goliath, leaders have invested in arms and armies, only to find that a "slingshot" in the hands of a "shepherd" can fell the mightiest warrior.

As we face the current War on Terror, history reminds us that we are not the first people to encounter the randomness of this kind of violence. For millennia, civilizations have placed their trust in "things" to make them more secure. Yet it seems more common that throughout the course of history, we have found ourselves enslaved, on the run from Pharaoh's armies, nomadically wandering in the wilderness, upended by famine, war, disease, economic and political dislocation. The relative material security of the Western nations since World War II has deluded us into thinking that life is about living on easy street. We forget that between 1880–1900 many European urbanites lived in fear of the anarchist bomber.

Living is risky, even without the immediate threat of war or terrorism. As humans, we experience suffering as well as joy. Across civilizations, the vast majority of people have been poor. It is only in the past century that any sizeable middle class has emerged. The eight-hour day was only won by America's unions in 1886.[2] Life for many in the industrial age in Europe was a hard reality. In 1890s Europe, for example, a cigar maker would earn 13 cents an hour and work 17 hours a day, seven days a week to support a family.[3] Many of us today can only look back with admiration for our ancestors who lived such a grueling existence.

So into the fray of risky living we go. The determination to place our trust in God, despite the upheaval of life's fortunes, is an act of faith.

For the writers of the biblical psalms, the challenges of life were no less daunting. Yet from that remote time during the Bronze Age come words still relevant today.

> You who live in the shelter of the Most High,
> and abide in the shadow of the Almighty,
> will say to God, "My refuge and my fortress,
> my God in whom I trust";
> For God will deliver you from the snare of the fowler
> and from the deadly pestilence;
> God will cover you with God's pinions,

and under God's wings will you find refuge...
You will not fear the terror of the night,
or the arrow that flies by day...
For God will command the angels concerning you
to guard you in all your ways.

— PSALM 91:1–4A, 5, 11 (NTP)

This psalm writer must know something about adversity. He knows about the snare of the fowler, deadly pestilence, terrors of the night, arrows, and the need for a fortress and a refuge. To hope for a better life and to not give in to despair takes courage. It requires trust. Looking at this psalm we can see that trust springs forth despite adversity. The psalmist trusts that God will command angels to "guard you in all your ways." In the midst of this adversity, God is a shelter, offering wings for protection.

In Psalm 23, arguably the most well-known psalm, the poet describes a pastoral scene. The writer has been led to green pastures and waters of peace; he has been bathed in oil and has received the bounty of a table spread before him. Still, he is led through a valley of the shadow of death and is seated at a table "in the sight of my enemies." The psalmists, writing about a God they trust, also speak of protection, which they seek from God, and about adversity from which God has spared them.

For some, to speak about wickedness, adversaries, and enemies feels disquieting. Aren't we beyond speaking of good and evil? Isn't that just an old dualism? Most students of psychology and spiritual growth accept that there is good and evil in everyone. Each one of us has our demons to wrestle with, as well as a capacity for unconditional love. It is important in times of conflict – whether within families, the workplace, community, or between nations – not to demonize those we are in verbal, physical, or armed struggle with. Human experience teaches us that a hug is more life-giving than a suicide bomb. Even people who have suffered abuse and who find it difficult to give and receive affection, value loving, human touch.

*Exercise:* **In God We Trust**

This exercise encourages you to explore the images and language you associate with trust, and with trusting in the Creator. Complete the following sentences to expand your connection with trust.

To me, trusting God looks like...
Trust feels like...
Trust sounds like...
Trust knows...
God created the quality of trust to show me...
God has saved me from...
I ask God's protection regarding...

Read what you have written and take time to form your thoughts into a psalm of trust.

## ENDNOTES

1 Bill Moyers, *Healing and the Mind* (New York: Doubleday, 1995), 344–345.

2 Barbara W. Tuchman, *The Proud Tower* (New York: The MacMillan Company, 1966), 77.

3 Ibid.

# 7

## Psalms of Wisdom

Since ancient times, literature from all cultures has concerned itself with wisdom. Sometimes this literature described wise thoughts and wise human behavior. Other times, it concerned the wisdom of the divine. The ancient poem *Salutation of the Dawn* originally written in Sanskrit, gives insight into the benefits of each day well lived. Here is my paraphrase.

Attend the Urging of the Dawn!
Behold this new Day!
It is Life, the essence of life.
In its short span rest all the
Circumstances and Truths of your Being.
The Happiness of Flourishing
The Splendor of Exertion
The Brilliance of Beauty
For the Past is a Memory,
And the Future a Distant Image
But Living Each Day with Passion makes
Yesterday a Source of Joy
and Tomorrow a Magnificent Opportunity.
Welcome with gladness this new Day!
This is the Greeting of the Dawn.[1]

These ancient words are used by a wide array of contemporary groups. In a search of the Internet, I found that it was used by personal business coaches, spiritual devotees of Sufism and Hinduism, student associations, and practitioners of yoga. The wide use of this ancient Sanskrit writing suggests many in our world are hungry for both ancient words and wisdom. When we hear words of wisdom spoken by the ancients, the simplicity of the message and its resilience through history anchor us to essential truths that sustain us in the midst of fad or fashion.

The following practical advice from a passage in Proverbs invites all to consider what it means to hold our peace – good advice for people known to put their feet in their mouths.

> Even a fool, if he holds his peace, is thought wise;
> keep your mouth shut and show your good sense.
>
> – Proverbs 17:28 (NEB)

The Roman philosopher Cicero observed that "the function of wisdom is to discriminate between good and evil." The poets of the Egyptian religions describe an early view of their god as being a god of all created peoples, not just the Egyptians.

> You care for the people of the lands, all of them;
> What Ea has created is wholly entrusted to you.
> Whatever has breath you shepherd impartially...
> You direct all the affairs of inhabited regions.
>
> – Hymn to the Sun-God[2]

In his book *How to Know God,* Deepak Chopra comments on the birth of a wise God, as people reach a greater state of awareness of the connectedness of all creation. He describes seven stages of God manifested in religious cultures. With the insight that God is wise, we no longer find it satisfying to believe that God is both quick to anger and sometimes merciful, that we live only by God's grace. We no longer find it satisfying to believe that God is almighty, requiring awe and obedience; or that God is peaceful, inviting us to listen to that small voice that enables us to maintain balance in the face of adversity. We only encounter the wise God when it matters to us that God is a redeemer. God is understanding, tolerant, forgiving, nonjudgmental, inclusive, and accepting.[3] This is a very different depiction of God than the one we find in the story of Noah, where God sought to destroy the earth and all its inhabitants. As people grow in relationship with God, more is demanded of God.

Wisdom literature found a welcome home within the Hebrew scriptures, a later development in the thought about the Holy One. This literature is found in the section of the Hebrew Bible called "the writings." Ecclesiasticus and The Wisdom of Solomon (or the Wisdom of Jesus Son of Sirach) are good examples.

It is not surprising that the psalm writers frequently discussed wisdom. Numerous psalms are devoted to reflections on wisdom. Psalms 15, 37, 49, 63, 73, 104, 111, 112, 119, 127, 128, and 133 all fall within the wisdom tradition.[4] Note the first psalm in the Book of Psalms.

> Happy are those who follow no evil counselors,
>> nor stand in sinner's ways,
>> nor sit with the insolent.
> Rather, they delight in the Holy One's teaching;
>> on that teaching they meditate day and night.
> They shall be like trees beside flowing streams,
>> trees that yield fruit in due season,
>> whose leaves never wither.
> All their work will prosper.
> Not so for the wicked!
>> They are like chaff blown away by the wind.
> Therefore the wicked shall not survive judgment,
>> nor sinners be among the just and faithful.
> Truly, the Holy One knows the way of the just and faithful,
>> but the way of the wicked shall perish.
>
> – PSALM 1:1–6

Like Cicero, the psalm writer is concerned about following the path of goodness and avoiding the ways of the wicked. This distinction is a sign of wisdom featured in many of the psalms from the wisdom tradition. Psalm 37 begins with the following advice.

> Do not be enraged over evildoers,
>> or burned up over those who work mischief,
>> for they soon wither like grass
>> and die off like green herb.
> Trust the Holy One and do good;
>> dwell in the land and live in security.

– Psalm 37:1–3

Psalm 15 tells us that we are worthy to dwell in the holy places of God when we speak truth from our heart, are not malicious, do not wrong a friend, do not speak against a neighbor, do not charge interest on loans, and do not take bribes. At first we may consider this advice too candid and perhaps even quaint. As citizens of the 21st century, we have been treated to many examples of corrupt government and business practice, and to unethical behavior among religious leaders and other professionals.

In his book *Thieves in High Places,* Jim Hightower describes the opulent tastes of one such professional in corporate America, former CEO of Tyco International, Dennis Kozlowski. Ranking up there with Enron, Global Crossing, Nortel, WorldCom, Imclone and other companies ridden by financial scandal, Mr. Kozlowski put a personal touch on the way he socked it to his company. Paying himself a $300 million a year salary while his company's stock was tanking, costing shareholders over $80 billion,[5] he had the audacity to purchase the following items for personal use and to charge them to his company as business expenses:

- a $6,000 shower curtain
- a $30 million, 15,000-square-foot waterfront estate in Boca Raton
- a $25,000 a month apartment rented in New York City
- a $16.8 million second apartment on Manhattan's exclusive Fifth Avenue (plus $3 million he spent to renovate it and $11 million more to furnish it)

- a third New York apartment...a $7 million Park Avenue co-op for his ex-wife
- an antique traveling toilet box for $17,000
- a $6,300 sewing basket
- a $2,200 wastebasket
- a $445 pincushion
- a $15,000 umbrella stand shaped like a poodle
- a $1 million 40th birthday bash in Italy for his wife.[6]

The extent of the corruption and debauchery is staggering. US taxpayers covered these "expenses," which Tyco wrote off as part of the cost of doing business, thus reducing their own company taxes.

The courts of the nations are filled with people accused of petty crime, violent crime, fraud, embezzlement, and conspiracy to harm, steal, or commit murder. Yet most of us seek out an honest living. We live out the words of Psalm 37 and "do not strive to outdo the evildoers or emulate those who do wrong." We hope that "like grass they soon wither, and fade like the green of spring." And so we get up each day with the simple intent to "trust in God and do good." For some, the temptation to cheat or to steal, to slander or to malign others in order to get ahead can be too great. Unless we have an ethical and moral compass to guide us, our will to persist on a path of justice ebbs away.

Within the wisdom tradition, Psalm 63 focuses on the wicked and the longing to do good. Here the psalmist longs to learn how to live a life of justice and righteousness.

> O God, thou art my God, I seek thee early
> with a heart that thirsts for thee
> ...whoever swears by God's name shall exult;
> the voice of falsehood shall be silenced.
>
> — PSALM 63:1, 11 (NEB)

## WHAT IS WISE? WHAT IS UNWISE?

Below is a list I wrote of 25 pieces of advice to increase or sustain wisdom.

- Take a moment to simply breathe and to notice your breath.

- Think of five things you are thankful for at the close of each day.
- Notice when other people resist your energy and spirit, and make choices about how to ask for respect from other people in your life.
- Have a daily encounter with the earth; walk for 30 minutes or more each day.
- Get involved in a spiritual community.
- Offer yourself through volunteer service.
- Do what you love.
- Cultivate humor at no one's expense.
- Harness your desires and direct your energy toward the things you delight in.
- Conquer fear with love.
- Tell others what you need.
- Listen more than speak.
- Notice where you feel in or out of balance; learn what brings out the best in you.
- Develop a relationship with a mentor who can affirm and support you as you grow.
- Dance, paint, write, or work with clay; find a creative outlet for your artistic side.
- Open your heart to yourself and to those around you.
- Meditate on compassionate action.
- Practice forgiveness and seek forgiveness; deepen your skills in reconciling with others.
- Adopt a simple lifestyle and de-clutter your life.
- Open yourself to the world of imagination, story, and myth.
- Listen to your heart and let it guide you to expressing your truth.
- Expose yourself to different cultures; allow yourself to cultivate curiosity and openness to people who are different from you.
- Pray.
- Learn the limits of knowledge and the beginning of wisdom.
- Learn your history – where you came from, your ancestors, and the story of the earth.

*Exercise:* Write your own list of 25 ways to cultivate wisdom. Write it as quickly as possible, allowing all the thoughts and fragments to come pouring out onto the page. Refrain from editing yourself and do not erase anything. Write without judgment and see what comes to mind. When you've finished writing, take a look at your list. Circle the five things that stand out the most.

Now the opposite: here is a list I wrote of unwise, illusory, or foolish actions.

- Start a fistfight with someone.
- Blame others for your own feelings of boredom.
- Interrupt people and cut them off in conversation.
- Gossip about everyone, even your "best friends."
- Faced with a chance to resolve a conflict, switch the conversation to something trivial.
- See people who have different skin color, gender, or class backgrounds as "other" and find ways to dominate them.
- View the earth and other species as things to subdue.
- Don't begin the day by saying "Good morning, God"; begin it by saying, "Good God, morning."
- When you notice you're in a depression or feeling melancholy, don't tell anyone about it and keep yourself isolated.
- Park illegally, often.
- Believe everything you are told by the media.
- Become ill to get attention or to be special.
- Keep very busy, work overtime constantly, so that family and friends hardly ever see you.
- Cheat on your taxes.
- Lie often about what you are doing to yourself and to others.
- Take everything for granted and be on the lookout for flaws in everything.
- Make a habit of staying up very late and sleeping in very late.
- Imagine that the world is a very hostile place and let that be your guiding Truth.
- Repress all sexual desire and nurture feelings of shame.
- Be a doormat; find ways to frequently apologize for yourself and for your behavior.

- Take everything seriously.
- Defend anyone who smears or slanders another, saying, "They really didn't mean it."
- Worry obsessively; listen to the police radio in your spare time.
- Hold grudges.
- Your top priority: more money, more material possessions, and shop 'til you drop!

After writing my two lists, I was aware of the stark contrast between a wise path and an unwise path. I was aware that a key difference between the first and second lists was that the second was full of attitudes and actions that would easily throw me off balance and prevent me from assuming an affirming stance in my life. The first list guided me towards those things that would help me to be attentive to the life within and around me.

In life we do not always know how things will work out. We stumble in the dark. However, being aware of what cultivates wisdom and what cultivates our neglect gives us something to ponder. It is said that whatever we give our attention to directs our thoughts. Being able to distinguish wise from unwise action has inherent value. The choice to ignore or neglect deeper reflection on what cultivates wisdom can impair our judgment and our ability to perceive things clearly.

William Stafford's poem "A Ritual to Read to Each Other" describes the costs of living life in a fog.

> For there is many a betrayal in the mind,
> a shrug that lets the fragile sequence break
> sending with shouts the horrible errors of childhood
> storming out to play through the broken dyke...
> I call it cruel and maybe the root of all cruelty
> to know what occurs but not to recognize the fact.[7]

The occasions for ignorance, arrogance, greed, jealousy, fear, and other things that can drive us against our better judgment are numerous.

*Exercise:* Write your own list of unwise paths and actions.

Review your two lists. In what ways can you best cultivate wisdom in your life? What unwise choices are most likely to tempt or ensnare you? Now complete the following sentence stems.

The first thing I notice about my wisdom list is...
The wisdom I practice in my life includes...
The wisdom I seek God's help with involves...
I can be fooled into thinking...
I've deluded myself when...
I lose my way on the path to God when...
The biggest challenges I face in following the ways of wisdom are...
The injustices in the world that bother me include...
My plea to God regarding corruption, slander, deceit, and other wickedness
    in this world is...

Take some time to review your completed sentence stems and notice what ideas and feelings have emerged.

In beginning a psalm of wisdom, you can try one of the phrases used in the biblical wisdom psalms. This is by no means a requirement, but it can be a good way to get started. Here are some opening lines you might consider using.

Do not strive...
Unless...
Happy are you...
How good it is...
With all my heart...
Hear this...

I have used the phrase "how good it is" to begin a psalm of wisdom, below.

How good it is for people to live together in peace,
how good to dwell in harmony.
It is like a soft pillow to rest your head
and never lose sleep.
It is like the hope you feel
when someone speaks to you for the first time
and you know that the word of God nestles in their heart.
It is like snow melting into the mountains
offering crystal springs to nourish a thirsty land.
There God will bless the people;
God will show favor and pour joy over each household.
The gifts of God are for the people of God,
for the people of God who seek peace and pursue it,
who do not wait for others to offer the hand of reconciliation.
The life of humans is really quite short.
Waking one day you will wonder, "What have I done with
my life?"
Do not wait for your strength to leave you;
Do not wait for the fire in your belly to burn to embers.
Do not waste your life on trivial matters.
Do not lose your soul to hearsay.
Do you not know the unguarded life is fraught with peril?
  You lose touch with your feelings.
  You ask others how you should feel.
Did God not create you?
Did God not give you a pulse, a spine,
a heart that beats, a tongue to talk.
All of you are wonderfully made.
Do not forget the gift of stillness
and God's voice that can be found in meditation.
The wise wake early and meditate on the ways of God.
The foolish follow after the gods of speed;

there is never time to rest.
Observe the Sabbath, whatever your day of rest;
keep it and honor your life;
your life is more than your work.
Do your work, then step back
and glorify God.

Now write your own psalm of wisdom. Consider: What is the big picture that God wants you to remember? What is the higher purpose, the long view, the insight into a situation that will keep you rooted in your relationship with God?

### ENDNOTES

[1] An original translation of the "Salutation to the Dawn" can be found in Elizabeth Roberts and Elias Amidon, *Earth Prayers From Around the World* (SanFrancisco: HarperSanFrancisco, 1991), 343.

[2] W. G. Lambert, *Babylonian Wisdom Literature* (Oxford: Clarendon Press, 1960), 126.

[3] Deepak Chopra, *How to Know God: The Soul's Journey into the Mystery of Mysteries* (New York: The Three Rivers Press, 2000), 102.

[4] Samuel Sandmel, ed. *The New English Bible with Apocrypha,* Oxford Study edition (New York: Oxford University Press, 1976), 569–665.

[5] Jim Hightower, *Thieves in High Places* (New York: Viking Penguin, 2003), 47.

[6] Ibid., 47–48.

[7] Excerpt from William Stafford's poem, "A Ritual to Read to Each Other," in *The Way It Is* (St. Paul, Minnesota: Greywolf Press, 1998), 75.

# 8

## *Historical Psalms*

Without a sense of history, all we have to guide us is the daily news broadcast or (even worse) "infotainment" program. Our life begins to reflect the reality Robert Bly describes in his book *Sibling Society*, where the only god is the god of speed.[1] We move from one event to the next without connecting the dots. "What was that Tanya Harding thing about?" we wonder out loud. "Who's Tanya Harding?" someone asks. "That's old news," says someone else; "Besides, did you see Janet Jackson on the Super Bowl?" A steady diet of spectacle and crisis can undermine our trust that the universe makes sense and supports our well-being.

As well, John and Jane Q. Public may know which ball team won the 2004 World Series, or be able to recall who played in the Stanley Cup final in 2003[2]; they may know the winner for Best Picture at the 1999 Academy Awards,[3] and may even be able to tell you which music group had the most, consecutive, number one hits in the 1960s[4]; but these kinds of statistics don't further our knowledge of the history of the world, or help us to find meaning as it unfolds before us. A number of authors have collected outrageous bloopers from university exams. For example, in his book *Non Campus Mentis,* Anders Henriksson cites exams handed into him in which students claimed that Christianity was just a cult until Jesus came along, and that Moses was part of the religion of Judyism.[5]

The world is filled with information. Satellite dishes can access over 200 TV channels. Libraries, the Internet, and schools offer seemingly unlimited opportunities for learning and integration. Yet among the fortunate who are able to get a post-secondary education, the integration of information can be shockingly sketchy.

The movie *Super Size Me* identified two factors that impede the advance of education. One is school lunch programs that serve mostly fast foods, and the other is lack of exercise.[6] At one point in *Super Size Me,* writer/director Morgan Spurlock meets some kindergarten children. He shows them a series of pictures of famous people. The children are stumped by the photos of George Washington and Jesus Christ. But they can all identify Ronald McDonald.

Buddhist philosophy says that whatever we pay attention to will fill our mind, what fills our mind will fill our words, and what fills our words will lead to action. For a nation raising a generation focused on Ronald McDonald, it may be harder to integrate the insights of history, government, democracy, ethics, and religion. A "supersized" population may not be able to take up the reigns of leadership, or grasp its roots as they envision their future.

In *A Distant Mirror,* author Barbara Tuchman explores the distant world of the "calamitous" 14th century. Marked most notably by the Black Plague, which killed one-third of the population living between India and Iceland, the 14th century was also rocked by schism in the church, war, taxes, rebellion, corrupt government, and crime. Tuchman's interest in the period was spurred by the parallels she saw between it and the tumult of the first 75 years of the 20th century. She comments on the wisdom that can arise from an understanding of history.

> The interval of 600 years permits what is significant in human character to stand out. People of the Middle Ages existed under mental, moral, and physical circumstances so different from our own as to constitute almost a foreign civilization. As a result, qualities of conduct that we recognize as familiar amid these alien surroundings are revealed as permanent in human nature. If one insists upon a lesson from history, it lies here, as discovered by French medievalist Edouard Perroy... "Certain ways of behavior," he wrote, "certain reactions against fate, throw mutual light upon each other."[7]

With a knowledge of history, we can begin to see patterns. We can see the behaviors at play when a government becomes corrupt. We can perceive foundational qualities that may be present in the expression of courage or folly, wisdom or denial. We can remember, for example, that Germany started World War II alleging that the Polish Army was amassed at the German border, ready to attack the German people with poison gas.[8] Many wonder about President George Bush's allegation that Iraq had weapons of mass destruction and posed a threat to the security of the United States, or Dick Cheney's claim that Iraq attacked the U.S. on September 11, 2001.[9] Yet, in 2004, U.S. weapons inspectors (known as the Iraq Survey Group) reported to Congress that Iraq had dismantled its chemical, biological, and nuclear arms programs in 1991 under U.N. oversight.[10] Since war is the final act after diplomacy has failed, intelligence used to assess the threat posed by another nation must be solid and verifiable before making a declaration of war.

We learn in a variety of ways, how to integrate what is being taught.[11] The history of a people can be glimpsed through poetry, songs, drama, and story, as well as through the writings of historians. These poems, songs, and dramas play an important role in enriching cultural memory. So, too, do the visual arts – paintings, stained glass, pottery, weavings, and other artistic media. In Medieval society, few people knew how to read and so sculpture and stained glass windows were a principal form of faith education. The windows and sculpture found at Chartres Cathedral in Chartres, France, are superb examples of biblical[12] and extra-biblical depictions.[13]

As a culture or religious community learns about its history, questions may emerge about how to discern God's activity *in* that history. Does history always reflect the will of God? Or might the will of God be something quite different than history portrays?

Could a crusader in Medieval times write a psalm praising God for the slaughter of the Islamic hordes? Could a member of the Central Powers (Germany, Austro-Hungary, and Italy) in World War I thank God for the slaughter of French, British, and American soldiers and citizens (or vice-versa)? Could a white segregationist write a psalm thanking God for frustrating civil rights legislation, or for keeping Klu Klux Klan members from prosecution? Or for keeping colored felons and suspected felons off the voting rolls in Florida in the November 2000 presidential election?[14]

Anthony Robinson, in a February 2003 column to the *Seattle Post-Intelligencer,* reminded his readership that Abraham Lincoln, whose moral stature looms large, refused during the Civil War to claim that God was on his side. Rather, he prayed that, "Stumbling and struggling through human life, trying to discern the signs of the times, we might perchance tilt from time to time toward God's side."[15]

Too often, leaders of nations gird themselves with the name of God and exact a terrible price on their enemies.

Can the psalm writer find any guidance for writing a psalm about God's acts in history? Does God smile on the oppressor and the oppressed equally? What foundation do the writers of the Hebrew Psalms lay? What premise guided them as they wrote about the saving acts of God? A closer look at the Hebrew Psalms will offer some clues.

In the historical psalms, the psalmists often describe how the people struggle to be faithful in their relationship to God. Sometimes the people respond faithfully to God; other times, they forget their promises. The psalmists also tell us that God shows favor to the people of God. God is concerned for the plight of the oppressed and the poor, the widow and the orphan. God blesses gratitude. God is impatient with those who complain that God has not done enough for them.

In the first two verses of Psalm 68, the writer says,

> God arises and God's enemies are scattered;
> those who hate God flee,
> driven away like smoke in the wind.
> Like wax melting at the fire,
> the wicked perish at the presence of God.
>
> – PSALM 68:1–2 (NEB)

The psalmist praises God for the liberation of Israel from Egypt, for the establishment of Israel in the Promised Land, and for the victories of Israel over various attackers in the ensuing centuries.

In writing a psalm faithful to the historical tradition, we do not have to write about the same subject matter found in the Book of Psalms. There are many periods of history which we can focus upon to hear a word from God.

In a speech to the Israeli Knesset, entitled "Israel Ignores Founding Principles," pianist and conductor Daniel Barenboim asked how the state of Israel could be indifferent to Palestinian suffering.[16] Barenboim is music director of the Chicago Symphony Orchestra and the Berlin Staatskapelle Orchestra. As a prominent member of the worldwide Jewish community, his observations of the Israeli government stirred the Knesset chambers and provoked reflection in newspapers across the country.

Born in Argentina, Barenboim grew up in Israel, arriving a few years after independence. I have rendered the comments he made in his speech into a contemporary plea that gives voice to his call to the compassion of the Israeli government.

> You, Yahweh, showed favor to the nation of Israel,
> its Declaration of Independence,
> transforming a rootless people into a nation of Israelis.
> Yahweh heard the promises of the new nation of Israel:
> "Israel will devote itself to its development
>     as a country, for the benefit of all its people.
> Israel will be founded on the principles of
>     freedom, justice, and peace.
> Israel will be guided by the visions of the prophets of Israel,
>     granting full, equal, social and political rights
>     to all its citizens, regardless of differences
>     of religious faith, race or sex.
> Israel will ensure freedom of religion,
>     conscience, language, education, and culture.
> Israel will pursue peace and good relations
>     with all neighboring states and people."
> Yahweh heard these vows and blessed Israel
> with many great achievements.
> Yet can the Jewish people, whose history

is a record of continual suffering and relentless persecution,
allow indifference to the rights and suffering of Palestinians?
Do not let us imagine a military solution.
Do not let us allow history to pass us by.
You gave me a piano to play,
an orchestra to conduct.
Listen, young musicians,
Jews and Arabs are making music together.
Together they transcend the limits of this present age.
Together they ascend to a higher sphere of the possible.
No longer are they enemies,
but fellow musicians in one orchestra.
Yahweh, help us move beyond words.
Touch us at the deepest places of human experience.
Help us cross all borders.
Help us imagine new spheres.
Let there be music in Israel.
Let there be music in Ramallah,
and let there be peace.

Barenboim's speech to the Knesset resembles some aspects of the historical psalms. A time period is recalled. In the first stanza, Barenboim lists Israel's vows in its declaration of independence, which crafts a picture of what kind of nation it will be. In the brief second stanza, he poses a question about the state of the relationship between Israel and the Palestinians.

The writer of Psalm 78 recounts the history of God's relationship with Israel. He describes the deeds of God done during Israel's unfolding. But he also punctuates this with remembrances of friction between God and Israel: "In spite of all, they persisted in their sin and had no faith in his wonderful acts" (verse 33); "Yet they tried God's patience and rebelled against him..." (verse 56).

Barenboim recalls a long tradition of thankful remembrance of the relationship between God and Israel. He identifies brokenness that needs repair and concludes with something in the relationship that can satisfy. Specifically, he envisions a future of harmony and points to signs of current goodwill.

The writer of Psalm 78 closes by recalling a time when God first chose David to be his servant. He also recalls that David shepherded his people with "singleness of heart and guided them with a skillful hand."

What Daniel Barenboim says to the Israeli Knesset is part of a struggle for the heart and soul of the state of Israel. Reaction in the Knesset reflected a range of views within government and opposition parties. Some praised Barenboim, describing his message as courageous and inspiring. Others condemned it as a slap in the face. Barenboim's statements are a kind of litmus test to rouse further discussion. Like the psalmists, Barenboim does not represent the voice of God. However, he puts forth a case, a view of history that points to both what is well and what is left unfinished in the life of the nation. The hope is that God can make use of Barenboim's controversial address in the Knesset, however partisan, to prompt some movement forward. Undoubtedly, the comments he made and the controversy they sparked will be added to as other people, both in Israel and in Palestine, offer their own important and contrasting views.

If a Palestinian Christian were to write a psalm reflecting on life in the Middle East since the establishment of the state of Israel, she might lament the dislocation of her people, the daily challenge of military checkpoints, the closure of marketplaces, the arrests and detentions, and the erection of the Separation Wall. She might also discuss suicide bombings, the Intifada, and the corruption that surrounded Yasser Arafat.[17]

A Jewish settler might write a different psalm about the unfolding history of Israel, stressing the need for military intervention by the Israel Defense Forces.

For each party in the Middle East, the struggle with God continues. All sides have suffered trauma from horrific violence. Not all Israelis are of one mind, and neither are all Palestinians.

Some historical psalms address God's acts in human history; others address God's activity in creation. In both types of psalms, one literary device is to contrast the promises of God with what God has done, and the promises of God's people with what they have done. Inevitably, there are several shifts in the mood within the psalm. The reader is told about the positive things that have happened. Then they hear about where there is trouble, from God's perspective or from the people's perspective. History represents an unfolding relationship with God. While there are achievements to be counted and gratitude to be expressed, historical psalms don't build to a crescendo of self-congratulation. Patience is needed from God, and from God's people.

Recently, I attended the swearing-in ceremony of a friend who was becoming a Canadian citizen. I listened to the words of instruction from the judge, and read *The Canadian Charter of Rights and Freedoms.* I considered what a challenge it is for a country to mobilize its citizens to protect the rights and responsibilities granted within a democratic society. The distractions of the modern world can erase any sense of urgency or need for disciplined engagement with the functions of democracy. Yet without the focused attention of the people, the fabric that makes a democracy strong can easily wear out. It seems that every generation needs to learn how to take responsibility for the governance of society.

While Canada has often ranked high on the United Nations index of desirable nations in which to live, Canadians should take nothing for granted. How people respond to their government is one aspect of the historical psalms. God, it seems, does not countenance listlessness or apathy. God rejoices when good leaders govern. God laments the corrupt and the cruel.

In the lecture Shirin Ebadi gave when she accepted the 2003 Nobel Peace Prize, she recalled her roots.

> I am an Iranian. A descendent of Cyrus the Great. The very emperor who proclaimed at the pinnacle of power 2500 years ago that "...he would not reign over the people if they did not wish it." And [he] promised not to force any person to change his religion and faith and guaranteed freedom for all. The Charter of Cyrus the Great is one of the most important documents that should be studied in the history of human rights.[18]

Ebadi goes on to recount the mission of the prophets of Islam to uphold justice. Knowing our roots, knowing our history, can be a powerful source of inspiration in the unfolding relationship we have with God and with our fellow world citizens. The visions we hold of how people should be treated are not simply a fashion of recent decades, but are rooted in the ancient longings of all people, everywhere.

*Exercise:* **Writing about God, God's People, The Creation, and History**

What period(s) of history do you want to bring before God? Think about the struggles between different groups of people, and between nations.

Describe where there has been justice or injustice. Who has been the oppressor, who the oppressed? Is something larger afoot here?

What have the different individuals, people, or nations to say on their behalf to God?

What does God see in the hearts and deeds of the people in this time in history – evidence of gratitude, patience, faithfulness, stubbornness, greed, hardness of heart...?

Describe what you believe God longs for in this situation.

Is there anything else God wants to express? Is there anything else the people want to express?

Now take some time to compose your own psalm to God about the historical period(s) you have chosen. Imagine what light God might shine on the situation.

## ENDNOTES

[1] Robert Bly, *The Sibling Society* (New York: Vintage Books, 1997), viii.

[2] The Boston Red Sox defeated the St. Louis Cardinals to win the World Series 4 games to 0. The New Jersey Devils defeated the Anaheim Mighty Ducks to win the Stanley Cup by a score of 3–0.

[3] *Shakespeare in Love,* staring Joseph Fiennes and Judi Dench.

[4] Joseph Edwards, *Top 10s and Trivia of Rock & Roll and Rhythm & Blues 1950–1973* (St. Louis, MO: Blueberry Hill Publishing Co., 1974), 496. The Supremes charted six consecutive singles to number one between August 1964 and December 1965 on the Billboard Hot 100.

[5] Anders Henriksson, *Non Campus Mentis: World History According to College Students* (New York: Workman Publishing Company, 2001), 9, 23.

6 Visit http://www.supersizeme.com for more background on this 2004 self-directed autobiography about Morgan Spurlock's quest to discover if "man can live on fast food alone." Morgan eats three meals a day at McDonald's for 30 days in a row, relying only on what is on the menu, accepting any offer from employees to supersize his orders, and tasting every item on the menu at least once.

7 Barbara Tuchman, *A Distant Mirror* (New York: Ballantine Books, 1978), xiv.

8 Jimmy Breslin, "Familiar Haunting Words," *Newsday,* Long Island, New York, 21 March 2003. In his address to the Reichstag, September 1, 1939, Adolph Hitler stated, regarding the problem with Poland and the Danzig Corridor:

On my own initiative I have, not once but several times, made proposals for the revision of intolerable conditions. All these proposals, as you know, have been rejected – proposals for the limitation of armaments and, even if necessary, disarmament, proposals for the limitation of war-making, proposals for the elimination of certain methods of modern warfare...

I am wrongly judged if my love of peace and my patience are mistaken for weakness or even cowardice...

This night for the first time, Polish regular soldiers fired on our territory. Since 5:45 a.m. we have been returning the fire and from now on bombs will be met with bombs. Whoever fights with poison gas will be fought with poison gas. Whoever departs from the rules of humane warfare can only expect that we shall do the same...until the safety, security of the Reich and its rights are secured.

9 "Bush Distances from Cheney on Saddam – 9/11 Link," *Sydney Morning Herald,* Sydney, Australia, 19 September 2003.

10 "Report: No WMD stockpiles in Iraq," *CNN,* October 7, 2004. "Saddam Hussein did not possess stockpiles of illicit weapons at the time of the U.S. invasion in March 2003 and had not begun any program to produce them, a CIA report concludes." See also "Powell says his assertions were wrong," *Seattle Times,* May 17, 2004.

11 Elaine de Beauport, *The Three Faces of Mind: Developing Your Mental, Emotional and Behavioral Intelligences* (Wheaton, Illinois: Quest Books, 1996), xxi–xix.

[12] Malcolm Miller, *Chartres Cathedral* (Hants, UK: Pitkin Pictorals Ltd., 1985). For a discussion of Gothic sculpture see pages 26–30 and 46–52. For a discussion of 12th-century glass, see pages 34–45 and 53–85.

[13] Ibid., 82–83. Chartres Cathedral features a Zodiac window with the 12 signs of the Zodiac together with a representation of Jesus.

[14] Alastair Thompson, "Diebold Memos' Smoking Gun: Volusia County Memos Disclose Election 2000 Vote Fraud" www.Scoop.co.nz, Wellington, New Zealand, Thursday, 23 October 2003.

[15] Anthony B. Robinson, "Nation Has Cause for Moral Reflection," *Seattle Post-Intelligencer,* Wednesday, 26 February 2003.

[16] Daniel Barenboim, "Israel Ignores Founding Principles: Conductor Asks How Jews Can Be Indifferent to Palestinian Suffering," *Los Angeles Times,* Friday, 14 May 2004. Reprinted from the speech Daniel Barenboim gave in the Israeli Knesset, 9 May 2004.

[17] Matthew Kalman, "Militants Put Arafat's Leadership in Jeopardy," *The Globe and Mail,* 19 July 2004. Kalman reports that "Palestinian legislators investigating allegations of corruption in the cement industry discovered that wealthy associates of Mr. Arafat, including his top financial advisor and the minister of trade, had facilitated the sale of cheap Egyptian cement to Israeli contractors building the hated security wall in the West Bank."

[18] Shirin Ebadi, "The Nobel Peace Lecture for 2003," *The Ploughshares Monitor,* Institute of Peace & Conflict Studies, Conrad Grebel University College, University of Waterloo 25 (Spring 2004): 17.

# 9

## Vows in Psalms

When I embarked on the journey that would eventually launch me into self-employment as a poetry and journal writing teacher, I attended a course through the Institute of Noetic Sciences near Santa Barbara.[1] My leader was a Radford scholar, Gay Luce,[2] the author of several books on personal growth that aim to help people experience deep joy in life. She had developed a program loosely referencing the Eastern chakra system as a way of understanding life's mysteries. During two ten-day retreats in 1999, I participated in an intentional learning community. As an intentional community, we established ways of being that enabled a high standard of respectfulness and love for each person involved.

One of the most powerful parts of the program was saying vows. By vowing to each participant an intention to speak from the heart, to remain guided by the wisdom of the heart, to allow compassion to be nurtured, and to be guided by compassion in service to each other, something radical emerged in the community. People felt a unity of purpose and interacted more effectively. There was little if any defensiveness, as people were able to make choices about how they wished to participate in each day's activities.

After the retreat, I wrote in my journal about this experience:

> It is quite amazing to me how much openness has been achieved in just a few days. This is not a sentimental sensation. The challenges

that people are taking responsibility to engage in are testing everyone's mental, emotional, physical, and spiritual stamina. Yet, there is this openness to learn and to trust.

My sense of why this is accelerating so smoothly is that we are a diverse group from more than one nation. We represent people from many walks of life, professions, religious and political beliefs. It seems that people have come willing to receive new teaching, and that includes being open to the novelty of new rituals, ways of belonging, and making meaning.

This is not for everybody.

Yet, the vows that we have taken have been very powerful.

How often are people in our society actually encouraged to take any kind of vow?

I think of weddings I have been to where couples have made vows to each other in front of the community of friends, relatives, and family.

I think, too, of the oaths that new citizens make when they apply to become a citizen of a new country. They publicly profess to stand for certain things, behave according to the laws of the land, and to exercise their citizenship responsibly. For new citizens, to declare an oath in public represents a culmination of a long process, an often difficult journey, to identify with a new country, its laws and customs.

Having taken these vows with complete strangers, I experienced several things that I do not want to forget.

1) I had to notice first if I could agree to the vow. I knew I would not speak out loud a vow that I did not agree with. There seemed no sense in reciting something with my tongue and believing something different in my heart. Thankfully the vows were consistent with my own beliefs. I learned that saying a vow involved personal consent and the lure of one's own heart to give voice to the words.

2) Speaking the vow out loud, I had to place myself in the present moment. I had to look at the person I was saying the vow to and send them my vow from my heart. I also had to be open to receiving their vows from their heart to my heart. Since there was no personal history

with any of these people, what was happening was not an exercise in discovering who I liked the most, or who could be my friend. It was an exercise of putting principles before personalities. If I could vow to one person that I would extend respectful communication to them, this would be a vow that I could extend to all people in the community. There is little power in a vow if we value and extend it differently with different people. The power of the vow is in its applicability to all the people in the community.

3) Having spoken the vow to each person in the learning community, I felt motivated to be true to my word. Having the focus of the simple vows I had made to the people in my community, I wanted to be my best. This was not a matter of trying to fake it until I made it, but of bringing a conscious intention for ethical behavior in all my relations.

4) Since the vow had been spoken aloud, and since I felt motivated to be true to my word, the vows were on my mind and in my heart. It was as if I was meditating on these vows so that I would be able to live them out. So often in the world outside of a retreat center facility, the distractions of life can make it harder to be mindful of the intentions we carry for ourselves and for our neighbor. Yet, in the retreat setting, there was time to keep a journal, to notice and be aware of interactions with others, and to bring forward the intention to realign with the vows whenever I felt I was losing my focus or tempted by carelessness. Vows were a reference point, moving me forward into each new day.

Though the community I was part of dispersed five years ago, I continue to be faithful to these vows. The spiritual connection with my co-learners has taught me a lesson in spiritual friendship – spiritual bonds are made stronger when people are able to ritually express their values and vision of themselves.

While communities may state creeds to affirm what they believe, a vow is always rooted in an active intention to behave a certain way with a specific group of people. Perhaps a vow comes from the heart more than a creed, which is much more rational. People coming together in intentional community generates commitment at a deeper level, which complements what reason affirms. This deeper intimacy often arises from speaking from the heart.

In Psalm 108, vows weave the psalm together.

> Holy One, my heart is steadfast;
>> my heart is steadfast.
>> I will chant and sing with all my being.
> Awake, lute and harp!
>> I will awake the dawn!
> I will thank you among the peoples,
>> hymn you among all nations.
> For your faithful love towers over the heavens,
>> your faithfulness over the clouds.
> O God, be exalted over the heavens;
>> may your glory cover the world.
> So your beloved may be rescued,
>> may your right hand deliver.
>> Answer me!
> You spoke in your sanctuary:
>> "I will exalt and divide Shechem;
>> I will measure off the valley of Succoth..."

— Psalm 108:1–7

In this type of psalm, the vow is expressed in the oft-repeated phrase "I will." This repetition also generates momentum and emphasis. There is rhythm. There is anticipation of what is to come, and familiarity, even while new images and ideas are added. At the end of Psalm 108 is a plea, followed by an affirmation of trust in God:

> O give us help in our danger;
>> human aid is useless.
> Through you we will act with courage,
>> while you stamp out our enemies.

— Psalm 108:12–13

An even clearer example of the psalmist making vows to God comes from Psalm 101.

> I sing of loyalty and of justice;
> to you, O God, I will sing.
> I will study the way that is blameless.
> When shall I attain it?
> I will walk with integrity of heart within my house,
> I will not set before my eyes anything that is base.
> I will hate the work of those that fall away;
> it shall not cling to me.
> I will be far from perverseness of heart;
> I will know nothing of evil.
> I will destroy one who secretly slanders a neighbor.
> I will not tolerate a haughty look and an arrogant heart,
> I will look with favor on the faithful in the land…
>
> — PSALM 101:1–6A (NTP, ADAPTED)

Whenever a vow is made before God, there is a deepened sense of intimacy. In the Hebrew Bible and Christian scriptures, the biblical characters often have intimate encounters with God in a natural setting. Jacob wrestles with God at a gorge by the ford of the Jabbok River. Moses meets God in a burning bush at Mount Sinai. Jesus is baptized by John the Baptist and is filled with the Holy Spirit in the River Jordan. Ezekiel receives a vision of God by the river Kebar. Elisha encounters the Lord while he spends a night in a cave at Mount Horeb. In Genesis 17:1, God appears to Abram and says "I am God Almighty." The literal rendering of "God Almighty" is "the God of the Mountains."[3] While God is also a God of the city, time and time again in the scriptures, the messengers, prophets, and chosen of God meet or have intimate encounters with the Divine in a natural setting. This is a common motif across faiths and cultures.

**Exercise:** **Guided Meditation and Composing a Vow to God**

In the meditation that follows, I invite you to seek God out in a natural setting. It may be by a beach, lake, river, stream, ocean, or marsh. It may be on a hill, a mountain, in a valley, gorge, or cave; in the desert, garden, forest, jungle, or alpine field – wherever you think you might encounter God. You may wish to go to a place you have already been, or somewhere new, or to a place that is suggested to you through the imagery in the meditation. You need not have a perfectly clear image of the place. Allow one to emerge as suits you.

Take a moment to be still. Gently breathe in, filling your lungs.

Now gently and slowly breathe out.

Inhale and exhale slowly several times, calming yourself.

Notice any areas of tension in your body and send ease and calm to those parts.

There is nothing for you to do. Simply enjoy this moment of being, breathing, living.

Imagine yourself in an appealing place in nature. A place with its own unique beauty. A place that is holy ground.

Look around. Notice the sights, the colors, the sounds, the scents, the textures that surround you.

In this beautiful holy place, God will appear before you. As you prepare for God's arrival, notice where you are in your life. What are the markers and symbols of your life's journey? In your journal, make a list of the things you are grateful for, allowing yourself to celebrate who you have become.

Now consider how you sometimes get out of alignment with God. Take a moment to list the ways you may sabotage or undermine your own good intentions. What old patterns, sometimes unbidden, cause you to be at your worst, so that you barely recognize yourself? Bring before God the places inside yourself, where you come undone; the people who "push your buttons," the situations that throw you off balance.

Re-read what you can celebrate about who you have become. Now re-read what you have written about the interior obstacles you face.

Consider who you want to become. Considering what brings out the best and worst in you, remember the words of Moses to the people of Israel when they faced a choice about who they were to be.

> Today I offer you the choice of life and good, or death and evil... I summon heaven and earth to witness against you this day: I offer you the choice of life or death, blessing or curse. Choose life and then you and your descendants will live; love the Lord your God, obey him and hold fast to him: that is life for you and length of days in the land which the Lord swore to give to your forefathers, Abraham, Isaac and Jacob.
>
> — DEUTERONOMY 30:15, 19–20 (NEB)

What choice lies before you? Describe this choice in your journal.

With this choice before you, use the following sentence stems to create your own vows to God. I have provided only three sentence stems below, but you may use as many as you need. I have also used the phrase "I will..." However, feel free to use a different phrase to repeat in your vow.

My heart wants to tell God I will...

My heart wants to tell God I will...

My heart wants to tell God I will...

Once you have written these vows down, reconnect with the beautiful holy place in your mind.

In the distance you can sense the presence of God.

What sights, sounds, and images appear before you as God comes to meet you?

God will address you and you will address God.

God wants to hear your vows.

Don't be shy. God knows what is on your heart and wants to grow closer to you. Knowing that God is genuinely interested in what you have to express, take a moment to speak aloud your vows to the Holy One. As you do this, allow for silences, allow for whatever needs to take place to honor your relationship with God and God's relationship with you.

When you have finished, imagine God making some vows to you. God has made vows before to the psalmists. It's not an unusual thing, yet it is a holy exchange. Write in your journal what God says to you.

Once God has finished communicating with you, imagine God inviting you to make a request.

Write down your request.

Upon hearing your request, God prepares to depart from this holy place. Imagine this departure any way you like. You and God can communicate anything you wish as you say farewell to each other.

Once God has departed, check in with your feelings. Take a moment to notice any shifts inside your heart. What do you take with you from this encounter with God?

Take a moment to write a description of your sense of trust as you reflect on your vows, the vows God has made to you, and your request that God has heard.

Now, re-reading everything that you have written, draw upon all that seems relevant to you as you compose your own psalm vow.

## Endnotes

[1] Founded in 1973, the website for the Institute for Noetic Sciences states: "We are a non-profit membership organization located in Northern California that conducts and sponsors leading-edge research into the potentials and powers of consciousness – including perceptions, beliefs, attention, intention, and intuition. The institute explores phenomena that do not necessarily fit conventional scientific models, while maintaining a commitment to scientific rigor. Through our publications, events, and educational media, we inform our members and the public about the frontier findings on personal and social consciousness and its relationship to the physical world."

[2] Dr. Gay Luce is a transpersonal psychologist, author of five books translated into seven languages, including *Body Time: Physiological Rhythms and Social Stress, Your Second Life,* and *Longer Life More Joy.* She is a three-time recipient of the American Psychological Association award for journalism. Dr. Luce also founded SAGE, a revitalization program that became the prototype for current work on aging. During her spiritual initiations, she spent a month in India with Gopi Krishna, joined Claudio Naranjo's Seekers of Truth, and worked extensively with Rinpoche Tarthang Tulku and other Tibetan masters. She is the founder of the Nine Gates Mystery School, and is a long-time friend and associate of Jean Houston, author of *Jump Time.*

[3] Samuel Sandmel, ed., *The New English Bible with the Apocrapha,* Oxford Study Edition (New York: Oxford University Press, 1976), 15.

# 10

## Royal Psalms

The "royal psalms" are those concerned with good government. The Hebrew people knew that having a good king was preferable to having a king who was corrupt, feeble, or, like Hamlet, incapacitated by indecision. The ruler of the 12 tribes of Israel needed to possess virtues that would embolden the people and enable them to prosper. I will return to this idea in a moment, but first it is necessary to address the theme of revenge, which is found in the Hebrew Psalms, especially in the royal psalms.

The language of revenge and vengeance found in some of the psalms is a stumbling block for many people. While it is one thing to thank God for "spreading a table before my enemies," it quite is another to advance hostility as a God-given path, as Psalm 21 does.

> Your hand will discover all your enemies:
> > your right hand all who hate you.
> In your anger you will make them a blazing furnace,
> > in rage, engulf them,
> > make fire consume them.
> You will destroy their offspring from the earth,
> > their descendants from all humanity.
>
> — Psalm 21:8–10

The history of the Hebrew people is filled with suffering, oppression, captivity, slavery, and fierce battles with Philistines, Canaanites, Moabites, Assyrians, and Babylonians. These people knew the trauma, devastation, and pain of warfare. They also knew feelings of rage, as invading armies brutally attacked their cities – Jerusalem, in particular – maiming and killing civilians. It is not surprising, then, that words of revenge and vengeance show up in the Psalms; it is a book that contains the whole range of human emotions. More importantly, *any* emotion can be brought before God. God is able to receive the whole range of our human experience and it is for that reason that God does indeed know us intimately.

Yet while we can learn from *all* the psalms, not every psalm will prove equally edifying. Psalm 23, for example, has proven much more enduring than Psalm 21. Psalm 23 acknowledges the presence of enemies, yet it focuses on the power of the presence of God to drive away fear, even in the valley of the shadow of death. While we may sometimes feel like exterminating our enemies, this emotional expression holds fewer possibilities for us as we seek to know the will of God.

In Judaism, the witness of the Psalms is tempered by the teaching of the Torah, considered the most authoritative text for guiding the faithful. Consider these verses.

> You shall not hate in your heart anyone of your kin; you shall reprove your neighbor, or you will incur guilt yourself. You shall not take vengeance or bear a grudge against any of your people...
> — LEVITICUS 19:17–18 (NRSV)

This line precedes the famous verse that Jesus quotes in the New Testament:

> You shall love your neighbor as yourself: I am the Lord.
> — LEVITICUS 19:18 (NRSV)

The Torah clearly teaches against hatred and revenge. This teaching is reflected in the following verse from Deuteronomy. Even though the Egyptians were regarded with bitterness and dread because of the slavery the Hebrew people endured at their hands, still the scriptures teach that

You shall not abhor any of the Egyptians, because you were an alien residing in their land.

— Deuteronomy 23:7 (NRSV)

The writers of the Torah knew that people were capable of nursing hatred towards their neighbors and towards people of other lands, be they Egyptians, Philistines, Moabites, or Babylonians.

Rabbi Harold Kushner recalls the words of Francis Bacon: "Revenge is a kind of wild justice, which the more men's nature runs to, the more ought law to weed it out." Then he remarks,

> In that one sentence, Bacon tells us four important things about revenge:
> - It is something that a lot of people are drawn to
> - It is natural, instinctive, not something we have to learn
> - It resembles justice, but is unlike justice in important ways
> - It is undesirable. It is natural the way weeds are natural, and if not checked, it will crowd out healthier emotions...[1]

It is important to keep in mind that all of us may harbor feelings of revenge at one point or another. Knowing this is helpful when reading the royal psalms. Someone in touch with their emotions can read Psalm 21 and identify with the vengeful side of him- or herself, while recalling the wise intention God has for our conduct with our neighbor, in times of peace *and* in times of conflict.

In her book *Psalms for Praying,* Nan Merrill has revisited the Psalms with a view to cultivating "a spirit of cooperation, co-creation, and companionship with the Beloved, rather than invoking a spirit of competition with God, other individuals and nations."[2] Her treatment of the Psalms is neither a paraphrase nor a translation. Instead, she reworks the Psalms in order to "open the heart to forgiveness, reconciliation and healing" – things needed to address the brokenness of our postmodern age.[3] In her reworking of Psalm 21, she shifts the focus from the outer enemies to the inner demons that take root in us.

You root out my fears: standing
firm beside me as I face
the shadows within.
Like a blazing sun your light shines.
My fears flee from your sight;
your fire consumes them.
Generations to come will sing to
your glory
in gratitude and joy for your
saving power.
For You put fears to flight, that
love and justice might reign.[4]

Merrill's reworking of the Psalms illustrates one poetic device – shifting the focus from the "outside" to the "inside" – a technique worth considering when writing new psalms. To give another example, Psalm 137:9 reads, "Happy is he who shall seize your children and dash them against the rock." Looking inward, we might ask, "What do we want to quash within ourselves in order to be available to God?"

Still, as we seek to write for a new day, there may be verses within the royal psalms that no amount of reworking can make palatable in the present moment. Not every scripture will speak to us at every point in our spiritual journey. While we may study the whole canon, inevitably certain passages will become touchstones for us, while others may be a source of constant alarm or bafflement.

In his book *Credo,* William Sloane Coffin writes about the cost and promise of knowing what is driving us. He remarks,

> Individuals and nations are at their worst when, persuaded of their superior virtue, they crusade against the vices of others. They are at their best when they claim their God-given kinship with all humanity, offering prayers of thanks that there is more mercy in God than sin in us.[5]

In grappling with the Psalms, we discover that they display both the worst and best of human intentions. Fear, guilt, hostility, despair, and contempt all lie woven within passages that may suddenly turn to love, forgiveness, peace, wisdom, gratitude, or trust. Each emotion we greet is one that is present, though perhaps dormant, within each of us. Jelaluddin Rumi was born in Balkh, Afghanistan, in 1207 CE. His poetry has evoked wonder, amazement, and inspiration in people around the world eight centuries later. In his poem *The Guest House,* he offers this wisdom regarding the emotions that arise within us.

> This being human is a guest house.
> Every morning a new arrival.
>
> A joy, a depression, a meanness,
> some momentary awareness comes
> as an unexpected visitor.
>
> Welcome and entertain them all!
> Even if they're a crowd of sorrows,
> who violently sweep your house
> empty of its furniture,
> still, treat each guest honorably.
> He may be clearing you out
> for some new delight.
>
> The dark thought, the shame, the malice,
> meet them at the door laughing,
> and invite them in.
>
> Be grateful for whoever comes,
> because each has been sent
> as a guide from beyond.[6]

In truth, we may require God's help to meet the challenge Rumi puts before us. Left to our own devices, we may be driven to commit unspeakable crimes. Like the psalmists, we may harbor shame, malice, and meanness, as well as joy and delight. By bringing to the Holy One the rawness of our emotions – "the dark thought," as Rumi coins it – we are handing them over to God's care. We may want God to crush our enemy, but God may hold a different vision. This is the risk we take when we bring ourselves before God with our curses.

Lack of honesty in our relationship with God is the cost of inhibiting or refusing to acknowledge the reality of anger, revenge, vindictiveness, malice, and other raw emotions. By bringing forth these difficult emotions, we move their energy to a spiritual outlet, acknowledging that some higher power needs to aid us in the midst of our distress or anguish.

In bringing our curses before God, we admit to God that we may be out of control. As we come perilously close to acting on thoughts of revenge, our psalms to God, curses and all, may provide relief, and may even help us see together with God the state we are in.

Consequently, each psalm can teach us about the energy of certain emotions. Revenge builds towards a vision of an enemy's extermination. Love builds towards wholeness and union with neighbors. The complexity of human emotion calls for wisdom.

Norman Fischer, a Zen-Buddhist monk, wrestles with the sections of the Psalms that curse the adversary, in order to discover their spiritual application for today.

> I felt as if their purpose was to arouse in the reader, chanter, singer, prayer a powerful emotional energy to overcome the selfishness, violence, anger, greed, confusion that is in all of our hearts and also in the world at large. These psalms make us acknowledge that it is there, they evoke it and raise up energy to overcome it… the enemies are others but also myself, my own inner violence, paranoia, etc… the cursing psalms bring our spirituality kicking and screaming right into even the most awful emotional states. I think this is good but also, as we both well know, very dangerous because people have for centuries used these cursing psalms as justification

for all sorts of nefarious stuff. I can say without any doubt that this is a mistake and a complete misunderstanding of what these psalms are all about. They are a passionate cry for goodness in the face of life's horrors, not a call to create further horrors.[7]

### *Exercise:* **Unsent Letter**

Writing a letter that you never intend to send can be a way of bringing forth emotions that need to be addressed in order to resolve an issue with a person or circumstance. Sadness, anger, confusion, incompleteness, or longing are some of the emotions that may be present. You may, in fact, be surprised by the clarity and power of the emotions that arise, but don't worry; no one is going to read this letter except you.

To prepare yourself, think of a person or a situation about which you feel a strong emotion. Perhaps you feel wronged. Perhaps you feel the situation involves wickedness, corruption, scandal, harm, or greed. Perhaps you feel you cannot forgive this person or situation. Search your mind for restlessness. Where are you ill at ease? What makes your blood boil? What makes you want to give up on something or someone?

Now take 15 to 20 minutes and write freely. Once you start, do not put your pen down. This is not an essay. You can make spelling or grammatical errors. Allow yourself to simply express your truth, your unbound feelings.

### *Exercise:* **Taking Difficult Emotions to God**

Re-read the letter you have just written.

Notice key words and phrases. Where is the energy in your writing? What ideas did you express? What are the key emotions? What are the images?

Now write a psalm bringing this situation before God. Be honest. Bring the feelings of being wronged: the sadness, the anger, the confusion, the longing, the desire for revenge, whatever has arisen from your unsent letter. Let God receive your complaint, your curses, your despair, your revenge. Place the matter in God's hands. Ask for whatever help you need from God.

## GOOD GOVERNMENT

We live in a world where more than one out of every six nations suffer from violent wars and civil unrest. To take for granted the need for wise and just leadership in government is a march of folly. This was something the psalmists never ceased to give attention to, as they knew the consequences of having a mediocre or corrupt king. The "royal psalms" speak of good governance and ask God to endow rulers with wisdom, justice, and mercy. In regards to the priority of military spending, the writer of Psalm 20, for example, envisions a ruler who concurs with this perspective:

> Some trust in chariots and some in horses
> but our trust is in the name of the Lord our God.
>
> — PSALM 20:7 (NEB)

The writer of Psalm 72 asks God to endow the ruler with qualities that will give rise to prosperity, justice, and peace.

> Give the king your sense of judgment, Holy One,
>   to a king's son your sense of faithful justice.
> May he judge your people faithfully
>   and give justice to your poor and needy.
> Let the mountains bring peace and prosperity
>   and the hills true justice for everyone...
> Indeed he rescues the needy who cry for help,
>   the poor who have no support.
> He has compassion on the poor and helpless,
>   and saves the lives of the poor.
> He will redeem them from injury and violence.
>
> — PSALM 72:1–3, 12–14A

Practical applications of the values expressed in this psalm are enshrined in the Magna Carta, or great charter, which has been *the* standard for just rule in Western Civilization since it was signed by England's King John in 1215 CE. The Magna Carta mandates that:

- The church has a right to be free from interference from the state, and to elect its own officials
- Widows are not required to remarry
- Law courts must have a fixed address where citizens can go to defend themselves
- Citizens are entitled to a fair trial, to know what they are charged with, and that witnesses to the crime must testify
- Citizens are entitled to a speedy trial, and not be left to rot in prison or beaten by government agents
- Citizens are entitled to freedom of movement within their country and to freedom from harm or threat by government agents
- Legal authorities are required to be knowledgeable of and not have contempt for the law.[8]

On October 18, 2006, President Bush signed the Military Commissions Act. "It was brought to Congress after the U.S. Supreme Court had ruled in June 2006 that the administrations plan for trials of detainees suspected of terrorism before military commissions violated U.S. and international law."[9] Under this law a president can designate U.S. citizens and foreigners as enemy combatants. They can be held without charge, put on military trial based on hearsay evidence, and sentenced to death based on testimony obtained through physical harm to witnesses testifying against the accused. "The bill...expands the definition of an unlawful enemy combatant...to anyone who has purposefully and materially supported hostilities against the United States...(and) removes a suspect's right to challenge his detention in court...a rule of law that goes back to the Magna Carta in 1215."[10]

Ancient psalmists commented on decisions by Israeli kings. A modern psalmist might give thanks for the intention in the Military Commissions Act to protect citizens from suspected terrorists. Another might plead for a legal guarantee of the right to know what you're accused of and to stand trial. Still another might lament.

In June 2004, scholars from around the world met at the University of Western Ontario to examine the theme "Why Neighbors Kill." One key finding is particularly worth noting.

One element that drives the fighting instinct is a history of injustice. In times of instability, groups look back at a "chosen trauma" that reminds them who their enemy is. Serbian leader Slobodan Milosevic, for instance, recalled a 14th-century battle in Kosovo that led to the occupation of Serbia by the Ottoman Empire, as added justification for "ethnic cleansing" of the Albanian Muslims from Kosovo.[11]

Since there is always the possibility that if we look back far enough we will be able to find a traumatic injustice in our history, it is imperative that rulers of nations be endowed with wisdom, so that they can manage *for the good of all peoples* the inevitable periods of instability that will rock their nations.

### *Exercise:* **A Good Ruler**

Think of the world leaders you admire today or from the past. What is it about them that stands out for you? What qualities do you seek in the leaders of your government? In the leaders of other nations?

Here is a list I made to get you thinking. Circle the qualities that are important to you and add your own. I would like my leaders to be...

| | |
|---|---|
| benevolent | hopeful |
| good communicators | humorous |
| compassionate | justice-seeking |
| consistent | passionate |
| courageous | patriotic |
| creative | peace-centered |
| curious | prosperous |
| decisive | responsible |
| exciting | respectful |
| faithful | risk-taking |
| fair | truthful |
| forgiving | uncorrupted |
| generous | filled with vitality |
| grateful | visionary |
| harmonious | wise |
| honest | |

Now, using your own list, write a psalm to let God know the qualities you seek in the leaders of your nation. What is required of world leaders, as they face the challenges of the 21st century?

## ENDNOTES

[1] Harold S. Kushner, *Living a Life That Matters* (New York: Anchor Books, 2001), 61–62.

[2] Nan C. Merrill, *Psalms for Praying* (New York: Continuum, 2003), vii–viii.

[3] Ibid., viii.

[4] Ibid., 35–36.

[5] William Sloane Coffin, *Credo* (Louisville: Westminster John Knox Press, 2004), 85.

[6] Coleman Barks, *The Essential Rumi* (Edison, New Jersey: Castle Books, 1997), 109.

[7] Meg Funk, "Norman Fischer's New Translation of the Psalms," *Monastic Inter-religious Dialogue,* Bulletin 69, August 2002, Washington, DC.

[8] See the British Library website on the Magna Carta. www.bl.uk/collections/treasures/magna.html

[9] Helen Thomas, "A Sad Day for America," *Salt Lake City Tribune*, October 18, 2006.

[10] Molly Ivins, "Habeas Corpus, R.I.P. (1215 - 2006)," Truthdig.com, Santa Monica, California, September 28, 2006.

[11] Olivia Ward, "Battling to Understand Our Genocidal Instinct," *The Toronto Star*, 5 June 2004.

# 11

## *Psalms for Holding a Vision*

Between 543 to 538 million years ago, something happened that scientists call the Cambrian Explosion. Animal life forms developed eyes. According to zoologist Andrew Parker's "Light Switch Theory,"[1] the development of eyes in predators launched the evolution of defensive shells and spines in prey, so that they could withstand attacks.[2] The Trilobite had the first eye on earth, called the compound eye. Before 543 million years, some species of Trilobite had light-sensitive patches, but none had eyes. Before that time *no species* had eyes! Humans have always had eyes, so we have often taken our vision for granted.

The change in animal life forms described by Parker can be a metaphor for any of us on our life journey. Are we using our vision? Do we see what's in front of us? Do we know where we're going? What's on our horizon?

Some say that the future is what you make of it. Others say the future is in God's hands. Some believe the future is pre-determined, while others contend that it is constantly being shaped by new actions. In this latter view, a random act of kindness may rekindle in us a will toward the good. A serendipitous encounter with new information may launch us on a new path in a relationship or a career. Trouble and tumult may lead us on to other, perhaps less desirable paths.

In Frank Baum's story *The Wizard of Oz*, Dorothy Gale is always getting into trouble with her aunt and uncle and their farm hands in rural Kansas. She imagines a place that is free of such troubles – a place beyond the sun, beyond the moon, beyond the rain. She concludes it must be somewhere over the rainbow. In this idealized world, Dorothy's troubles could all melt like lemon drops. When a twister drops her house into Munchkinland, Dorothy discovers a strange world of witches and talking scarecrows. In this new setting, Dorothy awakens to a new vision: "There's no place like home," even though it may have its problems. For Dorothy, the future she wishes for only comes true after she gains some wisdom about who she is and what matters to her.

Facing a completely different set of troubles, the writer of Psalm 46 seeks God's help. God is a refuge strong enough to banish the writer's fear. God is present in the midst of all kinds of tumult.

> God is our refuge and strength,
> a very present help in trouble.
> Therefore we will not fear, though the earth should change,
> though the mountains shake in the heart of the sea,
> though its waters roar and foam,
> though the mountains tremble with its tumult.
> There is a river whose streams
> make glad the city of God,
> the holy habitation of the Most High.
> God is in the midst of the city; it shall not be moved,
> God will help it when the morning dawns.
>
> — PSALM 46:1–5 (NTP)

At age 18, John Fox, a poet and author of *Poetic Medicine: The Healing Art of Poem-Making,* had his right leg amputated below the knee. He had a choice before him: to remain troubled by feelings of self-pity, or to accept both the reality of *"what is* and *help from God."*[3] In order to move from self-pity to a new level of acceptance, he wrote a poem called "Even to This." In this poem, he put fragments of his troubled thoughts onto the page. By the time he completed the last line, he experienced a breakthrough, and a vision of owning himself on new terms began to emerge.

### Even to This

What my thoughts have troubled about
all through the night after night!

It's so very scary
       sometimes
  I feel
           would rather
what's the worst that could happen?
because it just hurts too much

or having had enough of my own self-hatred
against myself, lonely is

nowhere else to go –
time to stop feeling sorry
for myself,

time to open my heart
even to this
and call to God

                                 – JOHN FOX

By letting his heart cry out, John Fox found a way to struggle with life's questions. He found room for his loss and launched a process of inner transformation, giving rise to a new vision of himself and of his relationship with God.

In the English alphabet, the Hebrew word for "was" is written HVH. The Hebrew word for "is" HYH, and the Hebrew word for "will be" is YHYH. The acronym for the holy Name of God is YHVH (also rendered as YHWH) – the one who was, who is, and who will be. No one can say what the future holds. However, we can attune ourselves to God's vision and seek to live a life that is delightful to God.

A vision of the future we are creating with God necessarily includes the ordinary events that mark our relationships, such as birthdays, anniversaries, parties to celebrate job promotions, retirement, and the like. These kinds of rituals focus our attention on the history of our relationships, our present enjoyment of them, and our anticipation of an ongoing future that is blessed. Living in anticipation of a future filled with hope and inspiration means celebrating these kinds of tangible events, but it also means having a broad vision that encompasses long-range goals for our relationships within our local and global communities.

Theologian Walter Brueggemann asserts that a distinctive contribution made by the Psalms is their view of God's justice for the human community. God's justice, he writes "is a characteristically Israelite concern that may correct or discipline a Christian restriction of the Psalms to privatistic, romantic spirituality. That is, *communion with God* cannot be celebrated without attention to *the nature of the community,* both among human persons and with God. *Religious hungers* in Israel never preclude *justice questions.*"[4]

New psalms also need to examine God's justice for the modern community. At the dawn of the 21st century, there are many questions to ponder regarding God's justice. What does God's justice require?

What vision might God seek for relationships between women and men; for humans and the ecosystem; for relationships between the world's richest and poorest nations; for refugees; for people living with HIV/AIDS, cancer, and other life-threatening illnesses; for children and youth; for the elderly; for the homeless, lonely, and depressed; for indigenous peoples; for nations torn by civil war and social strife; for the end of terrorism; for employees and employers; for religious leaders and their lay members; for relationships between members of different religions and between peoples of different ethnic backgrounds; for teachers and students; for health care; for animals; for cultural expression and creativity; for parents and children; for our relationship with God; for scientific research and the use of technology; for business practices and the management of our global economy; or the shape of our communication with each other?

As you read this list, you may think of other situations that require our prayerful attention. In our post 9-11 world, a number of voices have begun to emerge that may help create the future God longs for us to have. One story of the spirit at work comes from Albuquerque, New Mexico. Rabbi Lynn Gottlieb is the founder of Congregation Nahalat Shalom. Her congregation describes itself as "a spiritual and cultural center for Jewish Renewal in the Southwest. It affirms and supports discovery and exploration of Jewish identity, heritage, and the arts."[5]

One of the most significant contributions this congregation offers the Jewish community is a pilgrimage for peace. After the events of 9-11, Rabbi Gottlieb contacted a local lay leader at the mosque in town, Abdul Rauf Campos-Marquetti. She discussed with him the vision of a peace walk between the synagogue and the mosque. This tangible project strengthened the community of Albuquerque, through the dialogue among Jews and Muslims it engendered.

The peace walk itself brought out supportive members of many other faith groups, including Christians, Baha'i, Buddhists, Hindus, and Native North Americans. Each person in the walk wore white and carried signs that said "peace" in different languages.

The peace walks in Albuquerque have led to requests for Rabbi Lynn and Abdul Rauf to facilitate walks in cities as far away as Philadelphia, Pennsylvania, and Vancouver, British Columbia. As they travel, seeds of new relationship are being sown among Muslim and Jewish communities. Their work also provides a model for how the impulse to fear can be overcome and new relationships built on love and respect. Because people tend to fear groups that are historically different from their own, face-to-face communication is essential for understanding and peace.

In their presentation to a gathering at Synagogue Beth Israel in Vancouver, Rabbi Lynn said that both Jews and Muslims have suffered trauma in the past century. It is easy for a community to use its experience of trauma as a wedge or as a reason to be suspicious and fearful of another community. Yet the experience of suffering and oppression *can* be a powerful bridge for building relationships, when we listen with the heart.

At the outbreak of war in Iraq in March 2003, members of my home congregation, Canadian Memorial United Church, wanted to know what they could do to let Iraqi citizens know that they were in the hearts and minds of Canadians. Over a few short weeks, we raised $15,000 and assembled hundreds of personal care kits for families in Baghdad. These kits – which contained soap, shampoo, towels, combs, and toothbrushes – were all packed and shipped to

Iraq. In the face of war, the people of this congregation were grateful to take part in such a tangible act of kindness.

Stories like these often fall under the radar screen of big media. Yet beneath the constant reportage of fear, threat, and retribution lie stories of creative acts done by ordinary people trying to make the world a better place.

With war comes a clamor of accusations that stir up fears and instincts for protection and aggression. Once stirred, the winds of war carry the heat of furor into all fields of life. In his article "Going on the Peace Path," Michael Meade contrasts the path to war with the process of creating peace.

> …paths of peace develop more slowly… the paths of peace require the reinvention of sanctuary. Peace is a re-creation of refuge at the edges of conflict. Either path can require a great sacrifice on the part of individuals. It must have been a keen awareness of the differences between the war path and the paths of peace that caused tribal people like the Winnebago to elect two chiefs instead of one. Two chiefs could better represent the distinctly opposite paths that could open when threats to public safety occur. Being intimately connected to the ways of nature, they observed that most things appear two-sided, day and night, light and dark, upwards and down. People are two-handed, left and right; even the heart has internal oppositions pounding away moment to moment. And breath, the very vehicle of spirit goes in and out, out and in during moments of peace as well as when folks go on the warpath.[6]

The idea of two leaders of a tribe or nation holding such different positions, a war chief and a peace chief, sounds radical. Yet there is wisdom here. Most of us can understand the lure to defend against threat or attack. Most of us also know the longing for peaceful resolutions to matters of conflict. Having a department for peace and a department for defense would place both views firmly on the table in any discussion of what is required of a nation and its leaders.

Dennis Kucinich, a congressman from Ohio, ran in the U.S. Democratic primary for presidential nominee, in 2003–2004. He advocated the creation of a Department of Peace. Such a department, he said, would be "dedicated to peacemaking and the study of conditions that are conducive to domestic and international peace."[7] This vision was supported by 38 members of the U.S. congress in April 2003, as bombs were falling on Iraq.

War has claimed over 100 million lives in the past century. How do we find a way to tame war's excesses? What does God's justice require? What is God's vision for our world community?

Several psalms set forth a vision of a time when God will reign and the people of God will experience plenty, justice, harmony, and an end to suffering. Psalm 98 anticipates this future and the new songs of praise that will be offered at that time.

> To you we sing a new song
> For you are full of wonders
> Your right hand
> Your holy arm
> Has been victorious!...
>
> You remember your kindness and faithfulness
> To those who struggle and question
> To the ends of the earth
> Your salvation is revealed
>
> — PSALM 98 (ADAPTED BY NORMAN FISCHER[8])

The tradition of future vision extends beyond the Psalms across the Hebrew scriptures. In the Book of Exodus, God speaks to Moses.

> I have indeed seen the misery of my people in Egypt. I have heard their outcry against their slave-masters. I have taken heed of their sufferings, and have come down to rescue them from the power of Egypt, and to bring them up out of that country into a fine, broad land; it is a land flowing with milk and honey...
>
> — EXODUS 3:7–8 (NEB)

The vision God casts before Moses provides a powerful source of motivation and endurance. The horizon before Moses and the Hebrew people is strengthened with the hope of coming one day to a Promised Land. With this vision before them, they are able to suffer the present trials of life under the Egyptian Pharaoh, and to endure 40 years of wandering in the wilderness.

Here is a psalm I wrote, seeking the mind of God in the future's unfolding.

Let the earth rejoice at the wonders God has done.
May every heart beat with joyfulness and praise, for behold:
Truth reigns, formed from within, evident and compelling.
God has caused slander to flee,
and gossip melts under the brightness of integrity.
People have left their houses, they talk to their neighbors on the streets, unafraid,
virtual reality no longer dazzles them.
The minds of the people once captive to the oracles of fear,
are now bestowed with symbols stirring the power of imagination.
False gods have lost their power,
smear campaigns no longer hold sway.
Fear has gone into hiding,
while love stands firm, guiding the grateful of creation.
People have become as children.
Laughter is heard in the streets, the playground, the marketplace.
Playfulness abounds, joy springs forth to gladden the human heart.
The homeless have found a shelter,
the refugee a guest providing them sanctuary.
Greed has lost the power to manifest its poison,
generosity prevails and plenty abounds,
chronic fatigue, stress and anxiety are erased by vitality.
At the sign of dawn, people spring to life,
invigorated by the new community planted by God's hand.

Torture and violence God has banished.
> Everyone lives under the shelter of God's protection,
> clothed in dignity and honor.

People have remembered the blessings of the flesh,
> and no one is ashamed,
> freed from wounds of past violation and degradation.

People live respectfully in creation, as God has ordained,
> the panther, the marmot, the whale, the great blue heron,
> each has God sustained for all generations.

May God be praised,
> may justice roll like a mighty river,
> may all creation breathe deeply of God's gift of life.

### *Exercise:* Casting a Vision

Describe a common interest that people in your community, nation, or world might share.

What vision of the future might provide hope and promise for the world?

Psalm 98 says that Israel can rely on God's righteousness, constancy, love, and justice. What qualities do you imagine God will express in your hoped-for future? How might these be made visible and real?

The Psalms use a variety of images to describe the future – a lion lies down with a lamb, rivers clap their hands, God forgives and showers the earth with blessing. What images would you use to describe your vision of the future?

List any specific details that could give shape to a compassionate, daring vision. What does this vision look like, feel like, sound like, smell like, taste like?

Review any key words or phrases and then write your psalm of future vision.

## ENDNOTES

[1] Andrew Parker, *In the Blink of an Eye: How Vision Sparked the Big Bang of Evolution* (New York: Perseus Book Group, 2003).

[2] Ibid., 82–116, 142–170.

[3] John Fox, *Poetic Medicine: The Healing Art of Poem-Making* (New York: Tarcher/Putnam, 1997), 23.

[4] Walter Brueggeman, *Spirituality of the Psalms* (Minneapolis, MN: Augsburg Fortress, 2002), 59.

[5] For information about Congregation Nahalat Shalom in Albuquerque, New Mexico, visit their website www.nahalatshalom.org

[6] For the whole transcript of Michael Meade's article visit this archived web link: http://www.mosaicvoices.org/page.cfm?ID=54

[7] Jane Stebbins, "Udall Backs Creating Department of Peace," *Summit Daily News,* Vail, Colorado, 8 April 2003.

[8] Norman Fischer, *Opening to You: Zen-Inspired Translations of the Psalms* (New York: Viking Compass, 2002), 129.

# 12

## New Psalms
## and Other Sacred Poems

We praise you, O God, for the lives of Your servants
Wilfred and Muriel Smith
who reminded us that "the other" was none other than us;
who sang the praises of the poetry of our ordinary lives;
who taught us that we are bettered, and not lessened
by life's personal plurality.

— AMIR HUSSAIN

When I began *Writing the Sacred,* I envisioned the final chapter as a collection of new psalms and sacred poems. And so I invited writers from many faith backgrounds to write to the sacred – to speak of truth, trust, gratitude, wisdom, history, vows, and vision – and to send their compositions to me. Some of those I invited were seasoned writers, while others were novices to poetry and psalm writing. Amir Hussain's short poem, above, praising God for the lives of Wilfred and Muriel Smith[1] was part of an emerging variety I found as I opened each e-mail or letter.

The choices writers make when they begin to write is a testament to the infinite variety of starting places. A number of the people I invited to write felt intimidated by the prospect of being published. They did not see themselves as writers. What if what they wrote had already been addressed thematically by other contributors? What if their writing wasn't "good enough"? For one e-mail correspondent, I composed a "Psalm for Writer's Block," to show that even the feeling of being unable to start can be a starting point in itself.

### A Psalm for Writer's Block

Who am I, Creator, to write a psalm to you?
The very idea intimidates me
    and I feel paralysed.
I start to write it down
    and then I think about the others who are writing, too.
I compare myself to them.
    I judge myself.
Am I just a fraud?
    Do I have nothing to say to you?
What good are my words?
    They fall like withered leaves,
    lifeless, forgotten.
How can I express to you my essence?
    How can I tell you what I really want to express?
Without worrying about appearances,
    without worrying what others might think.
Help me trust again that You
    are at work in me as I begin to create.
Help me to let go of control of the outcome.
Let me do this imperfectly
    and move away from fear to love.

Thankfully, each of the writers eventually took up the task and sought to express something original.

Maya Khankhoje submitted a psalm for Quetzalcoatl, a Christ-like figure from the ancient Aztec/Mayan spiritual tradition (see Appendix D). The form of an Aztec psalm is distinct from a Hebrew psalm. Maya invites us into a world where the language is at first vaguely familiar, as seen in the short excerpt below.

Lord of all dualities
Dwelling beyond space
Before time
Faceless formless nameless
The one and the many
The void
You died and were born again
And again and again…

Leonard Angel's "In Letters of Light Engraved on Stone," invites a shift in perception and attention in its opening lines:

Why face
Jerusalem?
Face Me.

Dvora Levin greets the divine presence: "O thrumming endlessness, exempt from naming." Raheel Raza addresses God as "Lord of the Worlds and Master of the Day of Judgment." Celeste Snowber announces "the body declares the glory of God." Gay Luce and Deborah Jones invite readers to consider vows requiring "a lifetime's work" to achieve "a conscious way of living."

Questions that invite a deeper relationship with mystery appear in a number of the poems. Helen Carmichael Porter's list of questions leads us into a bully's lament.

Where were you God when I was an infant?
   Why weren't you there to protect me?
Why didn't you stop them from harming me?
   Why didn't you surround me with love?

Killian Noe, in her psalm "No more Us and Them," asks

How can I cross, without bridge
to follow or raft to ferry?

Must I strip, expose to dangerous deeps?
Plunge into raging rapids,
risk all in mystery?

Rhea Tregebov asks, "What makes you sure one thing is better than another?"

With each question we learn more about the heart and the journey of the writer.

Just as questions appear frequently in the psalms, so do requests. Susan McCaslin issues this invitation to God:

Patient One, fling your transformations
even to the outermost cul-de-sacs of suburbia.

At a time when demands weigh heavily and sap life energy, Dawn Rolke says

offer me again:
one simple garment
light pushing through
and a reason

The themes of these new psalms are as varied as the writers themselves. Susan Stenson offers praise for kitchens. Pamela Taylor gives thanks for her husband and children, while Sandra Hayes-Gardiner gives thanks for God encountered in the act of running. This is the sacred met in the ordinary; mystery encountered in the everyday.

The potentially destructive side of religion is explored in Bryan Teixeira's "Psalm 2004," where he cries out, "no more Messiahs, no more Buddhas, no more Prophets..." Like Teixeira, many who struggle with institutional religion still strain toward the light.

Mirroring the psalmists of old, several writers describe and observe the circumstances of their times. Derek Evans writes "of tragedy and desperation and cold, endless fear. The weight of helplessness, the shame of silence." Kathleen Adams laments:

...the soul murder continues,
the bloodbath continues,
the street fight continues,
the bombing continues...

Omega Bula raises issues of mortality, writing poignantly about the devastation of HIV/AIDS in Zambia.

In all of this, we often glimpse transformation in these new psalm writers. After letting go of a dead-end experience, Vicki Obedkoff affirms "I will begin again." Christina Baldwin sees a pattern in her call-and-reply relationship with God. She understands it as "our bargain and a fair exchange of grace."

Keri Wehlander perceives that God's faithfulness waits "with tenderness, ready to wash my fear away." This sense of God's presence is a catalyst for renewed relationship.

In the tradition of the Hebrew psalmists, many poets hold forth a vision of the future. Rabbi Zalman Schachter-Shalomia writes

May we come to honor,
Even in those whom we fear,
Your image and form, Your light
Dwelling in their hearts.

I am grateful to all of the authors who took part in this endeavor. Their enthusiasm reinforced my own. Imagination, novelty, creativity, challenge, tenacity, gentleness, and intimacy were just some of the many qualities present in the works I received. In the end, I believe we created a new vehicle to express our feelings, and new a way to offer them up to God. Read the poems, enjoy them, and be inspired by them to write your own.

## A Psalm of Lament

Lord, hear my despair!
I am crippled by the weight of my sadness.
How can it be that, in Your name,
   in the name of what is holy and true,

man turns against man,
   neighbor against neighbor,
   brother against sister,
   red state against blue state,
   nation against neighborhood,

in the streets of Fallujah and the West Bank
   and the towers of Manhattan
   and the monuments of Washington, DC
   and the caves of Afghanistan

drowning in rivers of blood in Your name?

In temples and churches and cathedrals and mosques
a single prayer rises:

"Deliver us from Evil
and exalt Your Holy name."

And the killing continues,
   the soul murder continues,
   the bloodbath continues,
   the street fight continues,
   the bombing continues,
   the jihad continues,

the insurgence continues,
the domination continues,
the crusade continues,
the intimidation continues,
the silencing continues,
the slaughter continues,
the mutation of rights continues,
the invasion continues,
the imperialism continues,
the reckless greed continues,
the rudeness continues,
the suicide bombing continues,
the terror continues,
the fear continues,
on foreign soil and in our own land.

A choir of voices risc as one:

"Deliver us from Evil, and
exalt Your Holy name."

and bombs explode
and mushroom clouds of hate
   blossom without end.

Lord, hear my prayer!
We are blinded by our arrogance.
We cannot find our way.
Deliver us from the Evil
   of our own misunderstanding,
Let us exalt the Holy name of Love.

— KATHLEEN ADAMS

Kathleen Adams is a bestselling author, speaker, psychotherapist, and visionary. Her first book, *Journal to the Self,* is a classic that opened the gates to the current cultural phenomenon of therapeutic writing. President of the National Association for Poetry Therapy from 2001–2003, she is the director of the Center for Journal Therapy in Denver, Colorado.

**In Letters of Light Engraved on Stone**
Why face
Jerusalem?
Face Me

I am your holy holy
innermost lamp oil
burning as your heart
is stone. Face
Me when you pray

I am far, so far
away, your parents whispered
egg and sperm, breathed birth

Jerusalem, Jerusalem, they
said, your substance
stonemaking clay, alive
and breathing, oh

inbreath and out-
breath, Light, the Light of stone
so far, so far away

Face Me when you pray

— LEONARD ANGEL

Leonard Angel is the author of *Enlightenment East & West, The Book of Miriam, The Unveiling, Eleanor Marx, The Plimsoll Line for the 21st Century, and The Silence of the Mystic.* He teaches at Douglas College in New Westminster, Canada.

**I Call**
I call.
Pause – oh trembling, doubting heart,
oh raging, hurtful mind –
and then, as ever and ever –
You respond.

I call.
You respond.
Easy to see you, God,
on the wing and keen of hawk,
or circle sun riding the mountain's teeth –
Nature so obviously divine.

I call.
And when You respond
not with Nature
nor ladders of angels
but in the gift of a human mirror,
how shall I receive?

I call – and my beloved delivers Your caress.
I call – and a neighbor lifts my load.
I call – and a stranger speaks your message.
Ah, I see that everywhere in everyone – You respond.

This, the original blessing –
how God slips through our fingers,
and rolls off our tongues,
and looks in each other's eyes,
and reaches with each other's hands.

God between us.
God within us.
God us,
partners of perfection and imperfection.

I call.
You respond.
You call.
I pause – to set aside my trembling, doubting heart,
to still my raging, hurtful mind – then
I respond.
This, our bargain and a fair exchange of grace.

— CHRISTINA BALDWIN

Christina Baldwin is internationally known as a founder of the personal writing movement. Through her classic text *Life's Companion: Journal Writing as a Spiritual Quest,* she has engaged tens of thousands of people in reflective writing. Her current book, *The Seven Whispers: Listening to the Voice of Spirit,* has been translated into Korean and Danish. She lives on Whidbey Island, Washington, USA.

**It's Like Planting Beans**
Enelesi is seventeen years.
Surrounded by relatives and friends
she is back at the Chingola Road cemetery
to bury Sonile, her six-month-old baby.
Born HIV positive
Sonile lies next to her father, Penjani.

Women, men and children burying the dead.
It's like planting beans.
Together they asked,
How long, Oh God, how long?

Together they sang,
How long, Oh God, how long?
Together they cried,
How long, Oh God, how long?

Next to Sonile lies Penjani,
tested HIV positive.
Lost the only paid job in the household
unable to fend for himself and his family
he went into a depression and died
leaving behind his pregnant wife.

Women, men and children burying the dead.
It's like planting beans.
Together they asked,
How long, Oh God, how long?
Together they sang,
How long, Oh God, how long?
Together they cried,
How long, Oh God, how long?

It is the fastest growing cemetery in Zambia.
Everywhere into the distance
children like Sonile are buried
their little mounds crammed close together
in a fast diminishing space
walked all over by mourners of the day.

Women, men and children burying the dead.
It's like planting beans.
Together they asked,
How long, Oh God, how long?
Together they sang,
How long, Oh God, how long?

Together they cried,
How long, Oh God, how long?

Enelesi, Sonile, Penjani.
They are the scars of poverty.
Enelesi, Sonile, Penjani.
Women, men and children burying the dead.
It's like planting beans.
Together they asked,
How long, Oh God, how long?
Together they sang,
How long, Oh God, how long?
Together they cried,
How long, Oh God, how long?

— OMEGA BULA

Omega Bula is the Executive Minister of the Justice Global and Ecumenical Relations Unit, and a former General Council Minister of the Racial Justice in the United Church of Canada. Born and raised in Zambia, Omega has traveled extensively around the world supporting and engaging in the struggles for justice. She writes her trip reports in this manner to enable the reader see the human face in the struggle for life.

**Luna – I**
Luna
Mother
Goddess
You who make the earth fertile, succulent, ripe!

Help me to be fertile.

Spread your seed within me,
   germinate it,
   nourish it.

Help me to slough off the dead husks of
   lethargy
   procrastination
   self-doubt.
Help the buds of new life shoot through the dry crust of my
infertility.
Moisten me with your glistening drops of moonlight.
Anoint me with your moonbeams.
Raise me up within your aura to be reborn with Christ as on that
Easter morn.
   New Life
   New promise
   Full of creativity
   Rich fertile soil
   Lush green growth
An abundance of beds and branches to flower and bear fruit,
   to redeem my weakness,
   soothe my spirit,
   refresh my soul.
To glorify your name, and, in turn nurture those around me as I
share your blessings.

— EMILY K. CHERNESKI

In 2002, after 30 years of city living and raising a family in Saskatoon, Emily Cherneski and her husband John relocated to the Fort Qu'Appelle Valley in Saskatchewan, Canada. They are presently living in community as volunteers at the Qu'Appelle House of Prayer.

### De Profundis

Men have walked upon the moon, Lord,
glorifying humanity and science.

But when, oh when, Lord,
will men and women learn
to walk here on the Earth
in the footsteps of your son,
doing as he asked,
to the greater glory of God?

We have added new words, Lord,
to hide the truth of death,
talking of collateral damage
ethnic cleansing, genocide,
just war, claiming for ourselves
self-defense and justice.

But when, oh when, Lord,
will we hear the old words,
and talk of mercy, forgiveness,
love, compassion, understanding,
sharing and caring?
Words You gave us to live by
shown by Your son,
who by his life
breathed life into these words.

Help us wake from our sleep,
and in your mercy:
Lord, hear our cry.

— MEL COATES

Mel Coates is a practicing Roman Catholic, blessed by a classical religious
education. He is well-versed in plain chant. For some years, he has been joining
a small group of Franciscan monks in morning prayer, reciting psalms and
canticles. He lives in Victoria, British Columbia.

## Grinding Time

These January days grow longer, but the cold is not yet spent.
Some say we will remember our past seasons as
"the pre-war years," "the decade of delusion."

No comforting horizon embraces this time.
These days of gloom
are numbered not named: "post-911."
Limitless,
the globalized frontier binds.

This is a grinding time.
Of tragedy and desperation and cold endless fear.
The weight of helplessness, the silence of shame.

At the northern tip of our lonely valley a family decides:
The burden of love and disability is simply and finally too much.
Holding hands, they lose the grip of life.

Ancient memories rage in sacred lands.
Differences define distinctions; distinctions prevail.
Children are destroyed.
We are told we are safer.

Enemies are executed in their sleep. Those who know
The sharp scent of hatred choose shelters of sulphur and disease
Astride the volcano,
rather than be refugees in a neighbor's land.

This is a grinding time. A new form struggles from the meal;
Like a secret prize, it will not be discerned or predicted.
Perhaps we will recognize it in birth, as it arrives, crowning.

Holy One, we crane our necks in expectation.
Over heads and around corners, we strain for a glimpse.
Bound together, we hope and pray, and try to keep
each other warm.

— DEREK EVANS

Derek Evans is Executive Director of Naramata Centre, and a former Deputy
Secretary General of Amnesty International. He is an Institute Associate of
the Wosk Centre for Dialogue at Simon Fraser University, and consults on
organizational development, conflict resolution, and human rights. He lives in
Naramata, in the Okanagan Valley of British Columbia, Canada. His most recent
book is *Before the War.*

*Take all your devarim*
*Your things, your words, your stuff,*
*And return to HaShem*

— HOSEA 14:3*

Take all your          **A**nger
Take all your          **B**rooding
Take all your          **C**ompassion
*And return to Hashem!*

| | |
|---|---|
| Take all your | **D**epression |
| Take all your | Embarrassment |
| Take all your | **F**oolishness |
| *And return to HaShem!* | |
| Take all your | **G**oodness |
| Take all your | **H**oliness |
| Take all your | Insight |
| *And return to HaShem!* | |
| Take all your | **J**oking |
| Take all your | **K**vetching |
| Take all your | **L**oving |
| *And return to HaShem!* | |
| Take all your | **M**ind games |
| Take all your | **N**euroses |
| Take all your | **O**bjections |
| *And return to HaShem!* | |
| Take all your | **P**ettiness |
| Take all your | **Q**uestions |
| Take all your | **R**ejections |
| *And return to HaShem!* | |
| Take all your | **S**adness |
| Take all your | **T**orments |
| Take all your | **U**nderstandings |
| *And return to HaShem!* | |
| Take all your | **V**ulnerability |
| Take all your | **W**ondering |
| Take everything you've | **X**'ed out |
| *And return to HaShem!* | |
| Take all parts of | **Y**ourself |
| Take your own | **Z**amboni |
| Take everything you don't need | |
| *And return to HaShem!* | |

— Hillel Goelman

Dr. Hillel Goelman is a professor at the University of British Columbia and is
Associate Director of the Human Early Learning Partnership (HELP). He lives
in Vancouver, British Columbia, Canada.

\*Author's note: In these words, the prophet Hosea appears to be simply urging the exiles from Judea to gather up their possessions, their *devarim,* and return to the land of Israel and the re-dedicated Temple in Jerusalem. On a deeper level, though, the prophet is also speaking of a more spiritual journey. *Devarim* is also the word for "words"; take your words of sadness, of exile, of loss, he is saying, and return to the Source of all life. These words are not the real "you"; like possessions they are temporary, ephemeral, blown away in the wind. You can discard these "things" (another translation for *devarim*), return to God, and in so doing return to your own true inner self.

This portion of the prophets is read in synagogue on the "Sabbath of Return," which is the Sabbath that occurs between the two major High Holy Days of Rosh HaShanah and Yom HaKippurim.

In this psalm I offer an acrostic based on this verse from the prophet Hosea. It is sung to a fairly upbeat and joyous rhythm; the words are intended to reflect the difficulty of the task of returning, but in a whimsical and accessible manner.

**The Rivers of Memory**
1. By the shores on the rivers of Memory
    There we laid us down and cried
    And hung our dearest melodies
    On the weeping willow's side

    Now vanished our horizons
    And lost each day before its rise
    There died our songs without singing
    Under fierce and foreign skies

2. Now those whose very living
    Makes a prison of our days
    They require of us our singing
    "Give us songs from your ancient ways.

For we can only plunder
Seeking life in the blooms we tear apart.
And your strains of an ancient freedom
Like an arrow, pierce the heart."

3. Every morning as I awaken
   I ask my God above,
   "Can a soul that lives in exile
   sing of life, sing of praise, sing of love?"

   This is my peace, my comfort,
   my prayers to you belong:
   In the silence of my yearning,
   May you lead me back to song.

4. By the shores on the rivers of Memory
   There we laid us down and cried...

— LINNEA GOOD

Linnea Good, sometimes called "the contemporary musical voice of The United
Church of Canada," leads workshops and concerts and works as a musical
liturgist, theological reflector, and educator. Her ninth album is called *Swimmin'
Like a Bird.* She was nominated for the 2004 Western Canadian Music Award:
Outstanding Children's Recording. She lives in Summerland,
British Columbia, Canada.

**Holy Ground**
Glory Be!
How did we get here?
Ask Arjuna

What road map did you dream,
immersing us in an astonishing classroom,
dancing lessons included;

newness of young guides
not yet disguising the depths of their deep rivers
yearning to vaster boundaries?

You, who were, all unknowing, in cahoots with Christ,
hands within hands
circle within circle
flung stones rippling, rippling:
Arjuna skips rocks over vast boundaries
past perceived darkness
past all his handicaps
into new light;
what he sees
waiting to be seen
church within church
big/little presbytery
birthing their dream, Christ's dream?

A young church riddled with paradox
and more love than most of us could ever dream:
where music and song and dancing and prayer become
holy communions;

where it is (sometimes) clear that
Jesus has taken Arjuna aside,
asking:
"Will you be Me, My Holy Fool,
Lord of this dance?"

Years tumble.
Patterns emerge.
Rhythms take root.
What is the lesson?
When young guides gather,

this same/not same
ever changing
circle of seekers

when music and singing soar
into and up through all our vast boundaries,
a Presence comes, almost tangible.

At this moment,
fine tuned
our ecstatic Arjuna
dances, dances
and
the circle knows
he has led us to Holy ground

Glory Be!

— MARY HATFIELD

Mary Hatfield served as youth worker for Quebec-Sherbrooke Presbytery of the
United Church of Canada from 1978–1997. Arjuna is one of the most spiritually
intuitive people Mary ever met through this work. Mary lives
with her husband, Carson, near Georgeville, Quebec.

### A Psalm of Praise: to the Runner God

Creator God
My awakening is yours
Even as my body resists
The leaving
Of night time warmth
My legs stretch into an early run
I fold myself into your rhythm
Feet on pavement
Feet on grass
Feet on gravel
Up and down
Feet on tree roots
Feet on stone
My feet dance the course
See you
At the bus stop
Entwining the chain fence
Waiting near the autumned trees

Suddenly
It is not
Your fence
Your trees
Your pavement
It's the you in me
That quickens inside my chest
And I know
I am
Your

Me.
And You and Me are one.

Over and over
I say it
As prayer
I
Am
Your
Me
My running self stops
And rests in you.
Tears
Trickle
Down
My
Running
Face.

You
Run alongside my heart
Claiming me – devouring me
Oh joy that bursts in my heart:
That
I
Am
Your
Me.

Astounding
Delighting
Astonishing
Surprising
Creator God

Beside me
Circling me
In me

All
Along

You –
The Runner God.

— Sandra Hayes-Gardiner
Sandra Hayes-Gardiner practices writing, running, and psychotherapy in
Williams Lake, British Columbia. She is a 57-year-old mother of three adult
children, "Gramma" to Flynn, and partner of 35 years to Lyall.

## A Psalm of Deliverance and Praise

You, my Beloved,
   are the source of my joy, my strength, and my praise.
When faced with overwhelming tasks
   and heavy responsibilities,
I came to you seeking wisdom,
   courage, and peace of mind.

You did not turn your back on me,
   but graciously welcomed me
   before your throne of grace.
Feeling vulnerable, with wavering faith,
   and with my own personal baggage,
   I presented my concerns before you.

I praise you, Lord, that you met me
   in my hours, days, and weeks of need.

The challenges were still present,
   yet You assured me
   that I had company for the journey.

With You as my companion,
   I walked the path that was before me.
Your faithful presence
   carried me through my tests.
Everything did not turn out as I wanted,
   yet all is well.

I am reminded that not my will, Lord,
   but may Your will be realised in my life.
I rejoice that Your grace is sufficient for me.
For your power is indeed made perfect in my weakness.

You, my Beloved,
   are the source of my joy, my strength and my praise.

                — PATRICIA L. HUNTER

The Reverend Dr. Patricia L. Hunter is an ordained American Baptist minister who lives in Seattle, Washington. Patricia works for the Ministers and Missionaries Benefit Board of the American Baptist Churches. She loves gospel music and worships at Mount Zion, a traditional Black Baptist church. She also enjoys gardening, baseball, and spending time with her family.

## A Psalm for Our Brothers
## Louis Riel and Anthony "Dudley" George*

*Two among many who were murdered for speaking the truth to power.*

Remember us, O God,
Your other daughters and sons.
Who received an equal share of the blessing
But not
The White skin and Good Christian character
Believed by some who possess them
To mark your favorite sons and daughters.

Remember us, O Creator,
When we speak truth to power.
Bless us when we are humiliated.
Be with us when we are persecuted and murdered.
You know, O Creator,
That nothing can kill truth
That all of Your creation is holy
And bears witness to your justice and beauty.

We thank you, O God,
For blessing us
With the darker skin
That you gifted to Your son.
Remind all of your children, O God,
That we all have all of the blessing.

— AMIR HUSSAIN

Amir Hussain is a member of the Department of Religious Studies at California
State University, Northridge, where he teaches courses in world religions. His
specialty is the study of Islam, focusing on contemporary Muslim societies in
North America. He serves on the steering committees of the Study of Islam
section for the American Academy of Religion. His forthcoming textbook is
entitled *Muslims: Islam in the 21st Century.* Amir emigrated to Canada from
Pakistan with his family when he was four and now lives in Los Angeles.

*Author's note: Louis Riel (1844–1885) was a Métis (mixed French and First Nations ancestry) leader in the Canadian Northwest, who helped to establish the province of Manitoba. One of the leaders of the Northwest Rebellion, he was hanged in Regina, Saskatchewan, in 1885. Anthony "Dudley" George (1957–1995) was a member of the Stoney Point First Nation. During a protest at Ipperwash Provincial Park near Sarnia, Ontario, George, who was unarmed, was shot dead by Ontario Provincial Police. He remains the only Aboriginal person killed by a police officer in a land claims dispute in Canada in the 20th century.

**A Psalm for Quetzalcoatl**
Ometecuhtli
Lord of all dualities
Dwelling beyond space
Before time
Faceless formless nameless
The one and the many
The void
You died and were born again
And again and again
Catapulting the spheres into orbit
Your blood dripped
From your celestial abode
Deep into our soil
Dyeing it green
Red silver sienna
Copper dawn
Crimson dusk
Midnight blue
Starry bright
Your breath blew
Mist clouds rainbows

Molten gold
Pomegranate juice
Liquid emerald
Sapphire fire
Caught in soaring wings
Drowned in bottomless oceans
Spread over grasslands
Glazed over high peaks
Tezcatlipoca
Smoking mirror father sun
You baked clay figurines
Into faces and hearts
Feeding them ripe corn
And roasted chocolatl beans
Fashioning stalwart
Warriors and women
And you sprouted peyotl
All over the land
For our seers and poets
To peer into your soul
Xochiquetzal
Blossom of all blossoms
Without your moist lips
The hummingbird
Would thirst for nectar
And lovers' lips
Would never meet
Without you
There would be
No flowers and songs
To mourn our dead
And cheer our living
And silence the screams
Of women at birth

Your fragrance
Stops our air from turning stale
Like the stifling depths of Mictlan
From where nobody returns
In which day and night are no more
And the warbler is silent
Quetzalcoatl
Plumed serpent
Astride the evening star
You had promised to return
Instead
Bearded strangers
Took on your shape
Descended upon us
From their floating houses
Trampling on our children
With their neighing four-legged
Metal-clad bodies
Putrefying our skin with their fetid pox
Torching our visions and our past
Reducing our understanding to ashes
Tearing apart our sacred cities
Tenochtitlan Tlatelolco Teotihuacan
And our steps to sun and moon
Strewing death and desolation
And we let them
Because we thought
You had come back
Where are you Quetzalcoatl?
Don your plumed garment
And ride the evening star
Cradle in your fangs
Our floating gardens
Our singing maidens

Our dancing warriors
Our bright birds
Our jade our obsidian
Our chocolatl
Come back
Bite your tail and swallow it
Quetzalcoatl
And close the loop
A new cycle begins

— MAYA KHANKHOJE

Maya Khankhoje's story "Journey into the Vortex," was recently published in
the anthology *So Long Been Dreaming: Postcolonial Science Fiction & Fantasy.*
Maya's other work can be found at www.MontrealSerai.com where she is
assistant editor.

## Psalm

O thrumming endlessness, exempt from naming,
    ignite the sparks to lift me from dreaming,
        take me deep in the mountains and into the abyss,
            to enter the truth of paradox.


May I learn there to balance compassion and justice,
    be a fulcrum for power and loving kindness,
        blend knowledge and understanding,
            to sip this nectar from wisdom's cup.


May I triumph in victory, know the grandeur of yielding,
    touch beauty and harmony, within and without.


May I embrace the sacred in every intention,
    including mine, yours, everyone's alike.

May I expand my vessel to hold the full essence,
     learn to give and to take with open hands.

May I linger only until the lesson is learned,
     fulfill my portion to repair this world.

May I ride the carousel of yearning, joy, and sorrow,
     encircle the nothingness, know everything is one.

May my soul be illumined by awe, exaltation.
     Angels, demons, *Shekhina\**, hello!

— DVORA LEVIN

Dvora Levin is a Canadian Israeli, recently returned from living in Jerusalem. She works as a management consultant with a focus on transformational leadership and conflict resolution. Having served as Director of the Cemetery and President of historic Congregation Emanu-el in Victoria, British Columbia, Dvora is now studying mystical Judaism, including Kabbalah. She writes poetry about her life pilgrimages and leads poetry workshops.
*Author's note: *Shekhina* is Hebrew for "Divine Presence."

## Psalm of the Nine Gates Mystery School

May we live deeply Vows made to each other,
"Right Speech, Purity of Heart, Compassionate Action."
Simple they seem, yet challenging us daily
To a lifetime's work, a conscious way of living.

I vow to you Right Speech –
Consciously hearing what I speak before sounds fly through the air.
Promising to be truthful and respectful,
To communicate, not manipulate,
To never speak to you, or about you,
In a harmful or disrespectful way.

I vow to you Purity of Heart –
Meeting you always with an open heart,
Without judgment or expectations,
Deceiving no one, not even myself.
Offering only love
Without attachment.

I vow to you Compassionate Action –
Moving beyond my need to "help."
Seeing you as fully capable,
Never broken, or "in need of."
Never becoming an enabler of your weaknesses.

I pray, Oh Highest Power,
To be willing... to be able... to vow this to all beings.
To have the ferocity of spirit this requires,
To act as a True Human Being.

— GAY LUCE AND DEBORAH JONES
Deborah Jones, Executive Director of Nine Gates Programs Inc., weaves
together into the very fabric of her work, 22 years of experience in corporate
America as well as studies with several master teachers from the world's
ancient wisdom traditions. She lives in Marin County, California.
Dr. Gay Luce is the founder of the Nine Gates Mystery School, created to aid
individuals seeking a deeper meaning in life, in the style of ancient, esoteric
mystery schools. She lives in Marin County, California.

**Psalm of the Open Secret**
O Holy One,
let your words sound in the crevasses of my speech.
Patient One, fling your transformations
even to the outermost cul-de-sacs of suburbia.
When the leaves shoot out their tender paeans,
wing my improbable transforming.

Though my root remains silent,
release my bloom into the attentive air.
Because you have praised the world into being,
I will praise you in the saturnine limbs of age.
Compassion and Praise will kiss each other
and all my works and days shall be beloved.
O Holy One, flexed in the arch of heron's neck,
anguished in the squeals of the farmed mink,
unnoticed in the fly swept from the ledge,
teach me your animal names,
bliss me your presence in the winged ones.

— SUSAN MCCASLIN

Susan McCaslin is a poet and instructor of English at Douglas College in
Coquitlam, British Columbia. She is the author of ten volumes of poetry,
including her most recent, *A Plot of Light*. Susan is the editor of the anthologies
*A Matter of Spirit: Recovery of the Sacred in Contemporary Canadian Poetry* and
*Poetry and Spiritual Practice: Selections from Contemporary Canadian Poets*. She
lives in Fort Langley, British Columbia with her husband and daughter.

**No More Us and Them**
Oh, Love, that will not let me rest,
on banks of river wide,
with currents swift.

Oh, Love, like heaven's hound, hunt me,
from separation, save me.

How can I cross, without bridge
to follow or raft to ferry?

Must I strip, expose to dangerous deeps?
Plunge into raging rapids,
risk all in mystery?

Go with me,
breathe through me,
until on water's edge
of shaded shore,
They run toward me.

And in their eyes
I see your light,
in their embrace find warmth.
'Til in their hearts, I'm home
where we are one.

— KILLIAN NOE

Rev. Killian Noe is co-founder of Samaritan Inns, a ministry that serves men
and women recovering from homelessness and addiction in Washington, D.C.
Along with others, she started the Lazarus Church in Washington, one of the
nine faith communities that make up the ecumenical Church of the Savior. In
1999, Killian co-founded the New Creation Community in Seattle, committed to
contemplation and action in the tradition of the Church of the Savior.

**God of Life, what do you want for me now?**
God of Life, what do you want for me now?
I am done weeping for what should have been, for what could
have been.
   I walk away wiser
         And go down to the river.
                I step into my kayak and push off,
                    grateful to go where Your living water flows.
             Your current carries me.

This boat will not be bullied; this ride not sabotaged.
    Here I read the river
        steering clear of rocks seen and submerged.
           I can choose in the moment to change course
    With surer and swifter strokes.

Look! The water turns red with Kokancc,
    inland salmon flushed crimson from their fierce struggle upstream.
        They heave their way home,
           Dying to spawn a new generation they will never know.
        A blessed struggle, a holy race, a flaming finish.

When I was small, swimming carefree days away,
    The red fish brought the end of summer.
        The air turned nippy as they charged by.
           But now I see Your grace in this flash of fish,
    A sign of new life coming from life spent.

I will begin again.
    Send the strength to swim upstream when You require
        for love and right relations' sake.
           Send like beings to share the Call, that
It may be a blessed struggle, a holy race, a flaming finish.
May it be a blessed struggle, a holy race, a flaming finish,
    A sign of grace for those passing by.

— VICKI OBEDKOFF

Vicki Obedkoff's passion for social justice comes from her Doukobor background and
30 years of United Church ministries. She loves picking huckleberries, taking nieces
and nephews to Naramata Centre in the summer, and playing piano for dances with her
band, the Lost and Found Girls.

## A Bully's Lament

Where were you God when I was an infant?
   Why weren't you there to protect me?
Why didn't you stop them from harming me?
   Why didn't you surround me with love?
Why didn't you stop the poison arrows of envy
   that filled me with fear and stopped me from growing?
Day and night I defended myself from my loved ones,
   Why did you not give me a refuge, a safe haven?

Now they assault me from within;
   The bullies are in myself,
They assail me with taunts and jibes,
   And show no mercy.
They tell me I am stupid, unfit,
   I will never be loved, I will never belong.

No matter what drug, drink, or food I take
   Or how much I sleep or work,
They find me when I am alone and quiet.
   No matter where I go, they come
And waste my energy.

They make me angry and mean
   I lash out at my partner, my kid,
I blow my horn at the intersection
   I am rude when the secretary gives me the wrong papers
I swallow my guilt
   And make dinner.

I am tired, God, of fighting them,
   I am weary of this battle

with these ghosts of my past.
I am fatigued with defending myself,
   I am exhausted from running away.
I am bored with living in this prison of fear.

I want to delight in your creation
   I want to be as whole and as free as a flower
I want to soar like a bird
   I want to dance like the wind
I want to take my place in the world
   that you have made
   I want to trust your universe.

I see your color in the sunset
   I hear your voice in the wind
I smell you in the fresh bread baking
   I touch you in the cat's fur
   I taste you in the glass of wine

I am your creation too
   You made me in your image
You gave me free will
   and a mind of my own,
   I am your handiwork.

Shut down the bullies in me, God,
   Close their mouths,
Shut their eyes
   Stop their ears
Keep them from assaulting me
   Blow them away.

I rise from my couch now
  and praise you
  the author of all,
  I celebrate myself
Your love surrounds me
  and lifts me up,
  In you I am secure.

                                — HELEN CARMICHAEL PORTER

Helen Porter grew up the youngest of four children in a United Church minister's family. In 1981, she became a professional storyteller. She has told stories in thousands of schools and made regular appearances on national TV and radio programs, such as CBC's *Morningside.* In 1990, she founded the National Storytelling Theatre, and, in 1996, created the popular *Bully Show* based on the stories she collected from students, friends, and her own life. Her current teaching includes a "Personal Narrative" course at the University of Toronto in the Creative Writing Department at the School of Continuing Studies.

## O God, Lord of the Worlds

O God, Lord of the Worlds
  and Master of the Day of Judgment
Advance our faith to the greatest perfection,
  keep us on the sacred path and guide us at every step.
Increase our good resolutions; do not let us be tempted by arrogance,
  let us be honored but do not let us fall prey to pride.

O God, we thank You for our health,
  for the land in which we live in peace,
for our children and our parents, for food,
  for our jobs that sustain us, for good friends.
  We thank You for being our resource and strength, when we are sad and in pain.

O God, we thank You for guiding us and ask You to help us absorb

and practice some beautiful and important lessons of life that you have taught us.

O God, help us learn that in order to receive love and compassion,

we must show love and compassion.

O God help us learn that humanity is one community

and that You are the Creator of all living beings.

O God, help us understand that we never have to do something extraordinary for You to love us,

we know You simply do.

Help us remember that the shortest distance between us is called a prayer.

O God, please accept our humble prayer today

and bestow Your blessing on each and every one of us.

Give us that which is good in this world and the next,

fill our hearts with love and compassion for our fellow human beings.

— RAHEEL RAZA

Raheel Raza is a writer, public speaker, media consultant, and interfaith advocate. A graduate from Karachi University in psychology and English, she moved to Toronto with her family in 1989. As a journalist, her interviews have included the royal family of Oman and Nusrat Fateh Ali Imran Khan. She has freelanced for *The Globe and Mail, Toronto Star, Khaleej Times* and *Gulf News.* In 2000, she received an award for excellence in writing from the Canadian Ethnic Journalists and Writers Club.

**You Who Keeps Me**
From scattered thought
    and solitary moment
    sea turtle emerges
    and makes slow passage
    knowing one way only

From twisted root – caution
From gnarled hand – a bird
From night – a song
From stone – this word:

Holy
    *holy*

When in confusion
thought turns in upon itself
and spirits fray,
offer me again:
    one simple garment
    light pushing through
    and a reason

Oh
you who keeps me
    keep me now
    in the wearied heart.

— Dawn Rolke

A United Church minster living in Saskatchewan, Dawn Rolke lives
with a deep sense of God's presence in and around her. During the final moments of
a retreat in the Fort Qu'Appelle valley in the fall of 2004, a long tiredness opened and
the words of this small psalm foung their way to her.

**Source of Time and Space**
Avinu Malkaynu!

From infinity draw down to us
The great renewal
And attune us to Your intent,
So that Wisdom, Your daughter
Flows into our awareness,
To awaken us to see ahead,
So we help instead of harm.

May all the devices we make use,
Be sparing and Protecting
Of Your creation.
Help us
To set right what we have debased,
To heal what we have made ill,
To care for and to restore
what we have injured.

Bless our Earth, our home
And show us all
How to care for her,
So that we might live
Your promise
given to our forebears
"To live heavenly days
Right here on this Earth."

May all beings,
Whom You have fashioned,
Become aware that it is You
Who has given them being.

May we realize that

You shaped our lives
And may each one who breathes
Join with others who breathe
In the delight of shared knowing
Of the great breath.

Assist us in learning
How to partner,
With family, neighbors,
And friends.
Aid us in dissolving old enmities.

May we come to honor,
Even in those whom we fear,
Your image and form, Your light
Dwelling in their hearts.

May we soon see the day when
Your House will be indeed,
The House of prayer
For all peoples,
Named and celebrated
In every tongue and speech.
On that day You will be one
And one with all cosmic Life.

Amen!

— RABBI ZALMAN SCHACHTER-SHALOMI
Rabbi Zalman Schachter-Shalomi is widely recognized as perhaps the most important Jewish spiritual teacher of the second half of the 20th century. He founded both Aleph: Alliance for Jewish Renewal, and the Spiritual Eldering Institute. He is Professor Emeritus of Religion at Temple University, and Professor of Religious Studies and former World Wisdom Chair at Naropa University. His books include *Paradigm Shift, From Age-ing to Sage-ing, Wrapped in a Holy Flame,* and *Gate to the Heart.* "Source of Time and Space" was originally written for *Prayers for a Thousand Years.*

**The Body Declares the Glory of God**

The body declares the glory of God
cells and joints
bone and blood
fingers and hips,
pelvis and lips
are filled
with the marrow of mystery.

Who can fathom the
smells of lavender
the taste of mango
the sight of red cedars
the feel of salt water on toes
the honey of love through flesh
or the torso extended in prayer?

My body knows the pulse
of the holy, softening
the broken heart.

My body knows the love
of the holy, rising in
the dancing limbs.

My body knows the center
of the holy, grounding in
the swinging hips.

My body knows the wisdom
of the holy, resting in
the breathing belly.

How spectacular is your love, Oh Spirit
that you would come in a body
be resurrected in a body
and let us know you through body.

You have made us with the
artistry of physicality
and we meet spirituality
   through flesh and form
gesture and glance
   rise and fall
   expanse and contraction.

May each fiber of our beings
touch the heart of stillness
dance into the night
with your love
and twirl in the light
of your great sky.

Hold us
   in the palm of your hand
   the folds of your breast
   the strength of your chest
and may your grace
ripple through our veins
that we may be
re/membered
in the embrace
of your love.

— CELESTE N. SNOWBER

Celeste Snowber is a dancer, writer, and educator who explores the poetics of embodiment through prose, poetry, and dance performance. She is presently writing a book on spirituality and sexuality. She is an assistant professor in the Faculty of Education at Simon Fraser University. She lives in Port Moody, British Columbia.

## This Kitchen as Proof

Because when there are eggs and we have another
    morning together, let there be omelettes,
    coffee, steam: no need to speak the word;
    we have the spoon, the knife, the fork, eat.

Because I know so often what you are thinking when
    you knead the bread, wait for it to rise, bake.

Because the waffles are on the plate. Butter slips into
    each square and over the top and into the hidden
    places. We add syrup from one of the two provinces
    we rarely think of except with buckwheat and flaxseed
    and walnuts and lemon glaze, Quebec, Ontario,
    no longer merely shadows, welcome maples, all.

Because the table is blonde oak from Denmark, the salt
    marks of the North Sea visible in the grain.

Because our kitchen has two sinks and a window above
    them and beyond the fence arbutus and fir curl
    in their own time toward the light.

Because look at us now. All kitchens have these things:
    pepper, salt, wine, milk, that last cup of tea. And praise.

— SUSAN STENSON

Susan Stenson loves her kitchen. Her poetry has been published in many
Canadian literary journals, most recently *Prairie Fire, CV2* and *Arc.* Her new
book, *My Mother Agrees With The Dead,* is forthcoming from Wolsak and Wynn.
She lives near Victoria, British Columbia.

## Raheem

Oh my Lord!
I have felt the caress of Your Palm
As You picked me up,
Lofted me across oceans,
And tenderly set me
In the one
Single
Spot
In this entire world
That would nourish the fragile shoots
Of my new found faith
And grow them
Into exuberant certainty
I have felt the touch of Your Breath
As You blew the Living Soul
Through my belly,
Into the stirrings of self
Growing there
Two precious humans
Sheltered in the warmth
Of my body's embrace
A gift
Given anew
Each day
Growing more generous.
I have felt the fire of Your Kiss
As You impassioned my soul
With Love
Wooing me with gifts
Beyond compare
Husband
Children
Words to win hearts
You are not the inconstant one

It is I who have faltered
Only to find
You have once again caught me in your Palm

— PAMELA TAYLOR

**Rahman***
How can I doubt your mercy, my love?

Let me not forget
The flamingo sun
Aflame in an evening sky
Streaked gold, fuchsia, violet

Let me not forget
The butternut moon
A round of ancient parchment
Hung like a Chinese lantern
Between elms

Let me not forget
The newborn calf with eyes of pure soul
The cobalt powder of a butterfly's wing
The exultant, exuberant growth of spring leaves
The curl of an infant's finger, the dimples in her elbows
The perfect symmetry of a single snowflake

Who, then, can doubt your mercy?

— PAMELA TAYLOR

Pamela Taylor has been a poet, novelist, and freelance writer for 27 years. She embraced Islam in 1988 and received her Masters of Theological Studies from Harvard Divinity School in 1992. Her work has appeared in a variety of Muslim magazines, including *Azizah* and *MuslimWakeUp.com,* as well as in the mainstream media. She is secretary of the Islamic Writers Alliance, and editor of their first anthology, *Many Voices, One Faith.* She lives with her husband, four wonderful daughters, and a terribly spoiled kitty in Indianapolis, Indiana.

*Author's note: Rahman is the name of Allah, which means "compassion" or "mercy" in an expansive, all-inclusive way. This is different from Raheem, the name of Allah that means compassion or mercy in an individualized, personal way. The phrase Bismillah ArRahman ArRahim is the Muslim's constant companion. It is used as a preface to each chapter in the Qur'an, as an integral part of the prayers, and as an invocation before anything a believer sets out to do.

### Psalm 2004

Praises to Heraclitus, to Hegel, and to Feuerbach.
Praises to Shankara, to Gandhi, and to Aurobindo.

Reclaim our possibilities from the heavens,
and pour ice cold water on the fires of hell.

Reject the hegemony of the priest and priestess.
Learn to build and walk your own path.

Religion is just one path before us, one mode of meaning-making.
New ones are emerging to replace it.

We stand on a cliff, and there is no bridge to the other side.
Let courage dawn in your heart and leap forward to embrace the
new day.

Leave the blood-soaked God hypothesis behind:
Truth calls us on.

No system is the final answer.
No word is the last word.

A God that can be owned by pyramid, or temple or church
is ultimately puny and no God at all.

The comfort of the believer is illusion.
At best, it may be a stepping stone.

They chant, "The Holy Book, the Holy Book, the Holy Book!"
But Wisdom and Truth are not frozen in the past and even the
best book has a shelf life.

Like flowers to the sun,
we strain towards the light.

We are not our minds, we are not our feelings.
In stillness, we find contentment.

Compassion is the child of stillness.
In silence we rediscover that we share one life.

Disconnection is illusion and the beginning of violence.
Connection is our natural state.

No more Messiahs, no more Buddhas, no more Prophets.
Celebrate Nature's exuberant diversity and variety.

To support the widowed and the orphan, to welcome the outcast,
to embrace the untouchable, to be a refuge to the persecuted:
these are the measures of our humanity
and the progress of civilization.

All is inter-connected.
Evolution is a healing process.

How can we express our inter-connectedness?
How can we honour diversity and variety?

And what lies beyond religion as we currently understand it?
Consider these things.

Above all, seek Truth and follow Justice.
Above all, seek Truth and follow Justice.

— BRYAN TEIXEIRA

Bryan Teixeira was born and grew up in Guyana. He has traveled widely and
has lived in Canada, India, the UK, and the USA. He is a former Roman Catholic
priest and was a member of the Capuchin Franciscan Order. A seeker over
many decades, he has explored Christian mysticism (Catholic and Protestant),
shamanism, yoga, Hinduism, and Eastern and Western philosophies and
psychologies. He lives in London, England.

**What Makes You Sure?**
What makes you sure
one thing is better than another?
I can walk down this sidewalk
with a bag full of groceries –
milk, butter, eggs, oranges, grapes –
I can walk all the way home
and never believe they were ever touched
by a single pair of human hands.
It's two days to Easter
and I can not buy lilies.
I can't quite place her death.
Walking back from the supermarket
I'm very careful of the eggs,
I was taught to be careful of the eggs,
never to break anything.
I'll break the skin of the grapes
against my tongue, but the eggs
I'll swallow whole.

What makes you sure?
I can live in one house my whole life
and never look out onto the yard
and see the bushes pressing their green paws
against the wind, avid, angry as I am.
Everything wants to live.
Me too.
Everything wants to live forever.

— Rhea Tregebov

Rhea Tregebov was born in Saskatchewan and raised in Winnipeg. She studied
English at the University of Manitoba, Cornell University, and Boston University,
and has traveled extensively in Europe and Latin America. She teaches "Poetry and
Translation" at theUniversity of British Columbia. Her five books of poetry have won
prizes, including the League of Canadian Poets' Pat Lowther Award (1994), and
the *Prairie Schooner* Readers' Choice Award (1994).

### Tree of Life

Ancient strength, this tree of life
water, breath and bone.
Each leaf linked to soil and star
no part stands alone.

Flight of an owl to form a branch,
scent of a rose to shape the trunk,
laughter of people to pattern the bark,
grace of a leopard to fashion a stem,
song of a whale to weave a root
no part stands alone.

May I revere this tree of life,
and see it as God's own,
walking each day, mindful of all
for no part stands alone.

— Keri K. Wehlander

You, O God,
sweet water of life
sparkle before me.

Parched though I am
I study you
from the shore of my desert.

Dancing, translucent river
fresh with grace
you open your arms wide.

I watch, filled with longing
but stilled by fear.
Uncertain. Unsure.

You, O God,
wait with tenderness
ready to wash my fear away
ready for me to swim in your love.

— KERI WEHLANDER

Keri Wehlander is an award-winning poet and the author of *Joy Is Our Banquet: Resources for Everyday Worship* and *Circles of Grace: Worship and Prayer in the Everyday.* Keri regularly leads retreats and workshops. She lives in Nanaimo, British Columbia with her husband, Curtis, and son, Aidan.

## ENDNOTE

[1] Wilfred Cantwell Smith (1916–2000) was one of the greatest scholars of religion in the 20th century. A Canadian, he founded the Institute of Islamic Studies at McGill University, the Department of Comparative Religion at Dalhousie University, and was a director of the Center for the Study of World Religions at Harvard University. He married Muriel in 1939, who remained his life-long partner and helpmate in their joint life's work.

# Epilogue

The Psalms and the invitation to write new psalms are a unique and relevant way to deepen our relationship with the divine. Life in the 21st century provides us with a vivid array of experiences. Work may be alternately pressured or satisfying. Family and relationships require our time and devotion. Our lives are filled with ordinary things such as making meals, commuting, gardening, exercise, health, education, managing finances and holiday plans. Out of these daily experiences come fresh occasions for and experiences of thanksgiving, lament, wisdom, trust, betrayal, love, forgiveness, celebration, promise, memory and hope.

Looking over the past week I wrote this psalm to make sense of a layered life.

> God, you've given me a week of trouble and beauty.
>> I marvel at the swans gliding on the lakeshore,
>> then I am sobered by a friend's stroke.
>> You give me an ordinary life.
>> Save me from boredom. Inspire me to take an interest in what
> You are doing
>> when I get my haircut,
>> when I patch plaster in the hallway,
>> or fold laundry.
> I am grateful that You rouse your people to be generous,

as many join together in song, walks, and benefits
to reach out to those devastated by disaster.
You gift me with new people to teach,
and show me again and again the desire for community,
learning and creativity.
Source of life, you fill the world with good things:
the taste of a crisp apple,
the smell of fresh lavender,
the sound of my guitar,
the sight of geese flying overhead
the touch of a friend's embrace.
Keep me from nursing anger when I am in conflict.
Help me to look beyond the dismissive comment
to know each person as you know them.
Help me to let go and open to you again and again.
Give me strength for each day,
and help me remember that
You made me in a body
and that I need to stretch and move.
Fill me with a wise and loving heart
that I may live each day with thanksgiving.

As I write from the everyday, I hope that your everyday experience provides for you raw material to you know yourself, and to move toward a balanced life and a deeper connection with *the presence.* May your own experimenting with writing sacred poetry help you to find a place within that ever-changing movement as you return again to the *mystery* within and behind this life.

# The Hebrew Psalms and Literature of the Ancient Near East

The Hebrew Psalms are part of the religious poetry, prayers, and hymns common to cultures in the ancient Near East. They are a beautiful and unique anthology of sacred writing. They reflect the message of a distinct community that sought to worship the Name above all Names.[1]

The Hebrew word for psalm is *mizmor,* which means a hymn sung to the accompaniment of a lyre. When the ancient rabbis named the anthology we know as the Book of Psalms, they called it *sefer tehillim,* meaning the "Book of Praises."[2]

Scholars speculate that the Psalms were written between 1000 BCE to as late as 200 BCE.[3] 2 Maccabees 2:13 states, "These facts are set out in the official records and in the memoirs of Nehemiah... Nehemiah collected the chronicles of the kings, the writings of prophets, the works of David, and the royal letters about sacred offerings, to found his library..." Nehemiah (ca. 445 BCE) is credited with collecting the works of David and the royal letters of the Persian kings. From the 2 Maccabees passage, then, it is possible to see that a Hebrew psalter ascribed to David was being created from the fifth century BCE. Canonized by the second century BCE, the collection of 150 psalms[4] we know today represents a high mark in poetic religious literature.

## LITERATURE OF THE ANCIENT NEAR EAST

In discussing the Psalms, it is important to consider their relationship to other writings in the ancient Near East.

The Sumerians, who had city states and fortified towns, represent the oldest known civilization. Sumerian language began, as many other languages did, as pictograms. In fact, the Sumerians developed the cuneiform system, which involved pressing wedge-shaped reeds into wet clay. (*Cuneiform* is Latin for "wedge-shaped forms.") According to Annie Caubet and Patrick Pouyssegur in their book *The Ancient Near East,* each pictographic sign contained images representing "an object or idea. But as early as 3000 BCE it began to shift from representing *things* to representing *sounds...* This new script allowed the complete transcription of language with not only its vocabulary but also its grammatical structure"[5] [italics mine].

Scholars of grammar suggest that grammatical structures may contain certain thought forms that transcend culture. In other words, just as our *ideas* can have an impact on how we use language, so too, the *structure* of language can influence how we express our ideas and feelings.[6] Some linguists, for example, point to European romance languages such as Portuguese, French, Italian, and Spanish as having a particular ability to access the language of the heart.

Over time, the form and structure of the sounds of letters and words created a medium through which poets and scribes across the Near East could communicate with their audience. The same is essentially true for us today – writers produce original works based on the literary framework their generation inherits. To say it yet another way, forms of communication do not simply drop out of the sky – they evolve over time.

A similar sort of process can be seen in relation to music. In just the past 75 years, music has evolved a great deal. For example, the blues music of the early 20th century gave rise to jazz, rock and roll, and the "Motown sound." And thanks to new innovations in sound technology, paired with the sheer number of new people writing and recording music, the outpouring of lyrical and musical styles continues to grow at a phenomenal rate.

Similarly, the Psalms were part of a much longer and slower wave of literary innovation and crafting of communication.

The Psalms were shaped by their context of the ancient Near East, which included both nomadic and settled communities. Commerce, war, and cultural festivals often spread new ways of thinking, communicating, and storytelling, including religious epics, myths, wisdom literature, poems, prayers, and hymns. This cross-fertilization of religious culture, and the shared origins of ideas created a context in which the adaptation of different religious styles of praise or lament flourished.

### SUMERIAN AND AKKADIAN LITERARY INFLUENCES

Given this cross-fertilization and the age and significance of the Sumerian literary tradition as noted above, it is not surprising that Sumerian influences can be seen in the Psalms and other Hebrew scripture.

The First Early Dynastic period of the Sumerians started around 2900 BCE, after the great flood. There is a Sumerian flood story that parallels the story of Noah and the flood described in Genesis 6–9.

The Akkadian Empire rose to power with the reign of Sargon of Akkad (ca. 2334 to 2279). It covered Mesopotamia. With the decline of Samaria, Akkadian became the language of diplomatic relations and trade in the second millennium BCE, until the Persians made Aramaic the official language. Akkadian is an Eastern Semitic language. There are a number of parallel stories, words, and phrases between Akkadian and Hebrew. The Akkadian creation epic *Enuma Elish* (the Akkadian name for "myth") has parallels with Genesis 1–2.

> When skies above were not yet named,
> Nor earth below pronounced by name,
> Aspu, the first one, the begetter,
> And maker Mummu Tiamat, who bore them all,
> Had mixed their waters together.
>
> — *ENUMA ELISH*, LINES 1–5[7]

Across all cultures of the ancient Near East there emerged epic myths and prose accounts of the origins of the world. Each of these accounts, which bear resemblance to Chinese, Haida, and other ancient creation myths, imagined a connection with a divine spirit or god(s) present from the beginning of creation.[8]

The legend of Sargon of Akkad (or *Agade*, in Sumerian) tells how Sargon was born of a priestess who gave birth to him secretly.[9] She put him in a reed basket in the river and he was carried downstream. A gardener found the baby inside the reed basket and raised him under Istar's protection. The child was called Sharru-ken, the legitimate king. Sargon grew up to become the cupbearer to the King of Kish. This story resembles the story of Moses in the Book of Exodus. The ending is quite different, however – Sargon overthrows the king and sets up his own kingdom at Akkad. In the Exodus story, of course, the Israelites are freed after the Egyptian plagues, and Moses leads his people across the Red Sea into Sinai in search of the Promised Land.

A parallel can be found in the Hymn to Aten and the psalms. This hymn is inscribed on the west wall of the tomb of Ay, Tell el-Amarna, in Egypt, the burial site of Pharaoh Akh-en-Aton. Written circa 1362 BCE, it reads,

> When you set in western lightland,
> Earth is in darkness as if in death...
> Darkness hovers, earth is silent,
> as their maker rests in lightland.
> Earth brightens when you dawn in lightland,
> when you shine as Aten of daytime;
> as you cast your rays,
> the Two Lands are in festivity.
> Awake they stand on their feet,
> You have roused them;
> Bodies cleansed, clothed,
> their arms adore your appearance.
> The entire land sets out to work,
> ...beasts browse on their herbs;
> trees, herbs are sprouting,
> birds fly from their nests,
> their wings greeting your ka,
> ...flocks frisk on their feet...
> they live when you dawn for them.

Ships fare north, fare south...
roads lie open when you rise;
...fish in the river dart before you,
Your rays are in the midst of the sea.
Who makes seed grow in women,
who creates people from sperm;
who feeds the son in his mother's womb,
who soothes him to still his tears.
Nurse in the womb,
giver of breath,
to nourish all that he made,
when he comes from the womb to breathe,
on the day of his birth,
You open wide his mouth,
You supply his needs...[10]

Biblical scholars have noticed this hymn resembles Psalm 104, as well as parts of the Mesopotamian epic *Enuma Elish*. All three use similar mythological language.

## BABYLONIAN, CANAANITE, AND OTHER INFLUENCES

The Psalms have found appeal across the ages and to diverse cultures. It is owed in part to the Hebrew people's exposure to different innovations within the evolving genre of the psalm.[11] These innovations in poetic expression were made by civilizations that predated the Hebrew people, as well as by contemporary civilizations giving literary expression to their search for the divine.

In F. W. Dobbs-Allsopp's view, the earliest examples of liturgical laments from the Old Babylonian period "retain much of the generic repertoire found in the historical city laments, but present them in a mechanical, often boring, repetitive, and unimaginative way."[12] Erica Reiner argues that Babylonian literature has not been appreciated as fully as other ancient literature for its contributions to the unfolding story of Western literature. It has often been considered more within the fields of "primitive" or "pre-logical" cultures and consequently has been precluded from much of literary history. Such is the fate of a "literature of an ancient and alien culture," with stories that are "difficult to apprehend by a taste sharpened on the classics and European literature."[13] The Hebrew psalmists, writing centuries later, had time to craft the literary style of the genres of lament and praise that existed within the world of the ancient Near East.

Resemblances also exist between Mesopotamian laments and Hebrew laments. F. W. Dobbs-Allsopp compares the "description of the destruction of the temple" in Psalm 74 with the Mesopotamian *Curse of Agade*.[14] Both describe enemies sacking the temple, planting conquerors' emblems in the shrine, victorious warriors' proclamations, the promise of the occupiers to destroy all the temples in the land, and the lament of the defeated people.

> Your oppressors have made an uproar in your meeting place,
>     and set up their own symbols.
> It seemed as if they had brought axes cutting away at trees.
> They hacked away at the carvings using axes and pikes.
> They set fire to your sanctuary,
>     and defiled your dwelling place.
>
> They said in their hearts, "Let us destroy them completely!"
>     They burned all God's shrines in the country.
> We see no signs; there is no prophet left
>     and no one knows for how long.
>
>                                   – PSALM 74:4–9

The *Curse of Agade* is a historical poem. It was written centuries after the fall of the Akkadian king Naram-Sin, to the invading Gutians, who lived in what is today the borderlands of Iran and Afghanistan. The poet blames the destruction of Agade (which occurred around 2279 BCE) on a prior attack by Naram-Sin's armies on the shrine to Enlil in Ekur. The poet documents this destruction:

> The gates of Agade, how prostrate they lay...
> The Holy Inanna leaves untouched their gifts;
> The Ulmash (Inanna's temple) is fear ridden since she has gone

> from the city, left it;
> Like a maid who forsakes her chamber,
>    the holy Inanna has forsaken her Agade shrine;
>    like a warrior with raised weapons she attacked the city in
>    fierce battle
> Enlil (God of the Air) has lifted his eyes to the mountains
>    and brought down the Gutians, a people which brooks no
>    controls...
> Over the places where your rites and rituals were conducted...
>    he has demolished the buildings with copper axes and
>    hatchets...
>    and desecrated the holy vessels...
> May the fox (who haunts) the ruined mounds, glide his tail...
> May your plains where grew the heart-soothing plants,
> Grow nothing but the "reed of tears,"...
> Who says "I would dwell in that city" will not find a good
>    dwelling place.
> Who says "I would lie down in Agade" will not find a good
>    sleeping place.

> — *CURSE OF AGADE*, SELECTED VERSES[15]

The poet's account would have been well-known across the Near East. The Hebrew psalmists would have become acquainted with the *Curse of Agade* during the captivity of the Hebrew people in Babylon, which covered a geographical area similar to the earlier Akkadian and Sumerian kingdoms. Is it possible that it was known to the writer of Psalm 74?

In 1928, a Syrian ploughman discovered texts in a tomb from the ancient city of Ugarit, a major Canaanite city destroyed around 1200 BCE. The Canaanites lived in what is present-day Lebanon, Jordan, Israel, and Syria. Translations of these texts revealed the "oldest complete alphabet" and a dialect "closely related to biblical Hebrew, as well as to Phoenician, Aramaic, and Moabite."[16] The Canaanite dialect discovered at Ugarit contained mostly consonants and few vowels – a feature of modern Hebrew and Arabic.

Canaanite poetic techniques were similar to those found in the Hebrew Bible. The major poetic device of the Canaanite authors was parallelism – within a verse, a single thought is composed in units of two or three lines (a bicolon or a tricolon). Poetic devices such as repetition, synonyms, or antonyms were also used. The following lines are a sandwich, with a double line as the bread and a triple line, or tricolon, as the filling.

> Let me tell you, Prince Baal,
>     let me repeat, Rider on the Clouds:
> Behold, your enemy, Baal,
>     behold, you will kill your enemy,
>     behold, you will annihilate your foes.
> You will take your eternal kingship,
>     your dominion forever and ever.[17]

Ideas about the Canaanite god Baal was very different from the followers of the God of Moses and of Abraham. Still, the language that found its way into the Hebrew Psalms contains striking similarities to the Canaanite text above.

> Behold your enemies, Yahweh,
> behold, your enemies have perished,
> all evildoers have been scattered.
>
> — PSALM 92:9 (NEB)

> Your kingdom is an eternal kingdom,
> your rule is forever and ever.
>
> — PSALM 145:13 (NEB)

The ancient peoples who traveled along trade routes were able to speak several languages. Multilingualism was a major asset for merchants, diplomatic messengers, scribes, and lawyers. While the history of the ancient Near East contains much war and plunder, it is also contains much commerce. This commerce provided fluidity across cultures, which allowed literary expressions to be shared.

## THE DIGNITY OF DIFFERENCE

The poems and prayers, addressed to one God or to many gods, testify to common themes people seek to express to the divine. These similarities exist in form and structure, poetic techniques used, meter, motif, and even theology. Yet the genesis of a certain genre, such as a lament, praise poem, or hymn to the divine, can have its origin within a certain culture, while the genre can arise independently in another. Tracing the "exact route by which a given idea passed from one author to...another," is not always possible.[18]

The Sumerians had at least eight principal deities. The Hittites had a thousand. A closer examination of the Egyptian religion suggests that while polytheistic sets of ideas emerged, the Egyptians also held monotheistic beliefs. "Egyptians believed in one God who was self-existent, immortal, invisible, eternal, omniscient, almighty...maker of the heavens and the earth, and underworld; the creator of the sky and sea, men and women, animals and birds, fish and creeping things, trees and plants."[19] The Egyptians were the dominant superpower of the time, the Hebrews their slaves. Still, the Hebrews' exposure to Egyptian civilization gave them one literary thread which in time lead to the emergence of the Psalms.

In his recent work *The Dignity of Difference: How to Avoid the Clash of Civilizations,* Rabbi Jonathan Sacks sees the need to consider how God makes use of difference as well as unity. Differences exist between peoples, cultures, faiths, economic and political systems. Sacks argues that we need to know why difference "exists, why it matters, why it is a constitutive of our humanity, why it represents the will of God."[20] Why is the world around us so diverse? Our natural, biological, personal, cultural, and religious contexts are all complex. This makes the world both creative and spontaneous. Coercing "an artificial uniformity in the name of a single culture or faith represents a tragic misunderstanding of what it takes for a system to flourish." Our differences enable each of us to contribute something unique and original. Yet the ancient "instinct going back to humanity's tribal past makes us see difference as a threat... Oddly enough, it is the market...that delivers a spiritual message: that it is through exchange that difference becomes a blessing, not a curse. When difference leads to war, both sides lose. When it leads to mutual enrichment, both sides gain."[21]

The Psalms are forged from the diversity of what it means to be human. The Psalms invite a wide range of religious moods, deepening contemplation into life's mystery. Poems, prayers, and hymns from other cultures – such as the Canaanite, Assyrian, Sumerian, Akkedian, and Babylonian cultures – have historical and literary interest. Like the Psalms, some of these are very beautiful and reveal insights into the minds and hearts of the ancient peoples who created them. Taken together, the Psalms and these earlier forms of sacred poetry sound the depth of longing in humanity's search for the divine across cultures and over time.

## ENDNOTES

[1] H. W. F. Saggs, *The Encounter with the Divine in Mesopotamia and Israel* (London: The Athlone Press, 1978), 3.

[2] Stephen Mitchell, *A Book of Psalms: Selected & Adapted from the Hebrew* (New York: HarperCollins,1993), xiii.

[3] Martin Rozenberg and Bernard M. Zlotowitz, *The Book of Psalms: A New Translation and Commentary* (Northvale, New Jersey: Jason Aronson Inc, 1999), xiv.

[4] "Most Greek manuscripts of the Psalter have 151, the last not appearing in any Hebrew manuscript of the Psalter until the discovery in 1956 of a Psalter manuscript among the Dead Sea Scrolls from Qumran Cave number xi." See Bruce Metzger and Rowland E. Murphy, eds. *The New Oxford Annotated Bible with the Apocrypha* (New York: Oxford University Press, 1994), 283.

[5] Annie Caubet and Patrick Pouyssegur, *The Ancient Near East* (Paris: Terrail, 1998), 146.

[6] F. W. Dobbs-Allsopp, *Weep, O Daughter of Zion: A Study of the City-Lament Genre in the Hebrew Bible* (Rome: Editrice Pontifico Instituto Biblico, 1993), 16.

[7] James B. Pritchard, *Ancient Near Eastern Texts* (Princeton: Princeton University Press, 1969), 119.

[8] For an examination of other creation stories see Virginia Hamilton, ed. *In the Beginning: Creation Stories from Around the World* (New York: Harcourt Brace Jovanovich, 1988).

[9] Caubet and Pouyssegur, *Ancient Near East,* 172.

[10] Pritchard, *Ancient Near Eastern Texts,* 370–371.

[11] Alastair Fowler, *Kinds of Literature: An Introduction to the Theory of Genre and Modes* (Cambridge: Harvard Unniversity, 1982), 154.

[12] Dobbs-Allsopp, *Weep, O Daughter,* 13.

[13] Erica Reiner, *Your Thwarts in Pieces, Your Mooring Rope Cut: Poetry from Babylonia and Assyria* (University of Michigan, 1985), ix.

[14] Dobbs-Allsopp, *Weep, O Daughter,* 155.

[15] Samuel Noah Kramer, *The Sumerians: Their History, Culture and Character* (Chicago: University of Chicago Press, 1963), 63–66.

[16] Michael David Coogan, *Stories from Ancient Canaan* (Philadelphia: The Westminster Press, 1978), 14–15.

[17] Ibid., 15.

[18] "Compare and Contrast: The Contextual Approach to Biblical Literature," in *The Bible in the Light of Cuneiform Literature* (eds. W. W. Hallo, B. W. Jones, and G. L. Mattingly; Lewiston: Edwin Mellen, 1990), 6.

[19] Sir Wallis Budge, *Egyptian Religion* (Toronto: Citadel Press Book, 1997), 17.

[20] Jonathan Sacks, *The Dignity of Difference: How to Avoid the Clash of Civilizations* (New York: Continuum Books, 2002), 21.

[21] Ibid., 22.

# The Influence of the Psalms in Jewish and Christian Communities

Between 400 BCE and 200 BCE, 150 psalms were collected and written down. The high regard for King David as a poet and musician within the Hebrew oral tradition lured many writers to ascribe to David newer psalms that were being added to this collection. Authorship of 73 of these psalms can, in most cases, be credited not to David but to that most famous author of them all – unknown.[1]

Distinct from the Law and the Prophets, the Psalms became part of the canon in that section of the Hebrew Bible known as Writings. They were used in Jewish liturgies as early as 180 BCE. Other Hebrew scriptures were written in subsequent years, but were not included within the canon of the Hebrew Bible. The *Pseudepigrapha,* for example, contains psalms and poems written in a style similar to those found in the Book of Psalms, as can be seen in my paraphrased examples below.

> Why do you slumber, soul, and do not worship the Creator?
> Sing a glad song to God, who deserves adoration.
> Sing and discover how the Creator knows you,
> for a worthy psalm to God comes from a joyful heart.
>
> – PSALMS OF SOLOMON 3:1–2

As the sun delights all who see it rise
so are You my delight, Creator;
Because You, Creator, are my sun, and Your rays revive me;
and Your light banishes all shadows from my face.
My eyes are Your possession,
and they see Your radiant day.
Ears I have gained,
and listen for Your wisdom.
The idea of wisdom I have gained,
and have existed completely through You.
I departed from the path of ignorance,
and moved toward You and gained abundant healing from You.
And fitting with Your blessing You give to me,
and fitting with Your splendid beauty,
You create me.

— ODES OF SOLOMON 15

These psalms are part of a larger body of writings that continued to be part of the living tradition of the Jewish community and its movement to express anew its praises to God. The *Pseudepigrapha* contains many examples of this writing within the early Jewish community.[2]

After the close of the biblical period, a curious contradiction occurred in the Rabbinic community. The habitual ways of writing new prayers and songs continued but were not acknowledged in the recorded *examinations* of scripture (midrash). James Kugel comments: "the ways of biblical parallelism are everywhere apparent in rabbinic prayers and songs yet nowhere do the Rabbis speak of parallelism or acknowledge it in their explanation or interpretation of biblical verses."[3] Notwithstanding, in the *Mishnah,* a record of the Jewish traditions of the first and second century, "there are more quotations from the Psalms than from any other part of the scriptures, save the Law itself."[4] The post-biblical Jewish community used the Psalms in temple ceremonies, celebration of the Passover, feast of Tabernacles, feast of Hanukkah, and days of public fasting.[5] The poetic style evoked in the Psalms and prayers contributed to the dominance of poetry in Jewish consciousness through to the Middle Ages.

Poets were of equal status to prophets. Shem-tob b. Joseph Falaqera (1225–1295 CE) spoke "of 'the prophets of song,' and poetic inspiration was sometimes identified with...divine inspiration."[6] Poetry was the recommended device to communicate anything of importance in the Jewish community. James Kugel remarks on medieval Hebrew poetry.

> It was used for everything – praise of patrons, shaming of enemies; love songs, wine songs, occasional verse of all kinds; religious songs incorporated into the synagogue service; learned treatises and polemics; all these found the new poetry their natural medium.[7]

The medieval Jewish community also rediscovered the meter of biblical songs. For years, many Jewish biblical commentators had scowled at the repetitions in the parallelisms of the Psalms (and elsewhere) as redundancies. Kugel says that the eventual willingness of these commentators to "countenance repetition and restatement as such, and to view them as essentially emphatic forms of expressions, was an important step" in the widening acceptance of poetic expression in community life outside the Temple.[8] This relearning of the poetic structure of passages and books within the Hebrew Bible enhanced the proliferation of poetic devices in the synagogue. By the Middle Ages there were "15 types of songs sung in the Temple, and a corresponding 15 possible meters in medieval Hebrew."[9]

The richness of the Psalms may explain why they have been used so extensively in Jewish worship since the early days. In contemporary Judaism, the Sabbath is observed in Jewish communities around the world every Friday at sundown. There are over 20 psalms read over the course of that night and the following day. The Jewish prayer book, *Siddur,* draws frequently upon the Psalms and is influenced by their poetic structure.

## The Psalms in Christian Communities

Clearly, the Psalms were a source of inspiration to the first Christians and had an impact on the early Christian community. In fact, A. F. Kirkpatrick has counted 93 passages from the Psalms quoted in the New Testament.[10] Certain passages of the New Testament also contain *patterns* of writing similar to those found in the Hebrew Psalms.

The use of parallelism is, of course, one of the defining features of the Hebrew Psalms. Parallelism is evident where subsequent lines of poetry build on the opening line in some way. Sometimes the subsequent line or lines look back to the first and restate it for emphasis. Sometimes the second part expands the thought in the first line. On other occasions, the second part represents a contrasting statement or a reversal of the first.

The *Nunc Dimittis* in Luke 2:29–32 is one example of this kind of pattern usage, as is Mary's *Magnificat* in Luke 1:46–55:

> My soul magnifies the Most High
> and my spirit rejoices in God my savior;
> who has looked with favor on the lowliness of God's servant.
> Surely, from now on all generations will call me blessed;
> For the Mighty One has done great things for me,
> and holy is God's name.
>
> — LUKE 1:46–49 (NTP)

The opening lines of the *Magnificat* offer another example, where the second line, "rejoice, rejoice, my spirit, in God my savior," builds upon the first by expanding on the thought "Tell out, my soul, the greatness of the Lord."[11]

The use of the Psalms in the Jewish tradition at the time of the new Christian religion and their frequent reference within the new Christian scriptures contributed to a reliance on the Psalms in Christian worship. The result has been that the appeal of the Psalms within the Christian church's liturgical life has spanned 2000 years and has found resonance across continents, cultures, and schisms within the church.

One of the places where the Psalms quickly found a home was with the ancient Celts. The evangelical message brought by Christians to Ireland was made easier by similarities between the Psalms and the Celts' own writings. For example, the repetition of the first person singular, I, as a device to invite the hearer into the poem was familiar. While the voice is different in its specific content, this structural device is used in both Psalm 101 and in ancient Irish poetry. Notice the similarities between the psalm and the verses from 200 BCE ascribed to Amergin from the *Book of Invasions:*

> I sing of loyalty and of justice;
>     to you, O God, I will sing.
> I will study the way that is blameless.
>     When shall I attain it?
> I will walk with integrity of heart within my house,
> I will not set before my eyes anything that is base...
>
> — PSALM 101:1–3 (NTP, ADAPTED)

> I am the wind which breathes upon the sea,
> I am the wave of the ocean,
> I am the murmur of the billows,
> I am the ox of the seven combats,
> I am the vulture upon the rocks,
> I am the beam of sun,
> I am the fairest of plants,
> I am the wild boar in valour,
> I am the salmon in the water,
> I am a lake in the plain,
> I am a world of knowledge,
> I am the point of the lance in battle,
> I am the God who created the fire in the head.[12]

It is easy to imagine the Psalms appealing to the new converts in 6th-century Ireland. St. Patrick was said to have repeated the whole Book of Psalms daily. The rhythm and poetic structure of the Hebrew Psalms contained many similarities as well as novel poetic devices, which appealed to the Celtic culture.

Another fascinating story of this kind of appeal comes from the first Christian mission to northwestern China, in 635 CE. The Church of the East brought the teachings of Jesus to the Emperor of the Tang Dynasty. There, the church's mission created a viable Christian community that co-existed within the Tang Dynasty alongside Shamanism, Confucianism, Taoism, and Buddhism. A Taoist

Christian text from approximately 780 CE reads in part:

> Let us praise Allaha – Great Father and Mysterious One
> Let us praise the Messiah – his Supreme Son
> Let us praise the Holy Spirit, who witnesses divinity...
> Let us praise the Constantly Bright Supreme Happiness Sutra
> The Sutra of Origins
> The Sutra of Subtle Peace and Happiness
> The Sutra of Heavenly Treasures
> The Sutra of Psalms...
> The Acts of the Apostles according to Luke
> The Sutra of Paul's Dharma, and of Zakarias...
>
> – THE SECOND LITURGICAL SUTRA: LET US PRAISE[13]

That the "Sutra of Psalms" was praised in a liturgical Sutra suggests that the Psalms were known and used in the liturgical practices of the Taoist Christians. Indeed, the story of the emergence of the Taoist Christian community from the fifth to 11th centuries in northwestern China is a fascinating example of cross-cultural communication and influence.

Here is another sutra from the 8th century, which shows the kind of Hebrew parallelisms found in the Psalms. The units of two lines are coupled together – the first line makes a statement and the second builds upon it.

> Everything praises you, sounding its true note,
> all the Enlightened chant praises.
> Every being takes its refuge in You,
> and the light of Your Holy Compassion frees us all.
> Beyond knowing, beyond words,
> You arc the truth, steadfast for all time.
> Compassionate Father, Radiant Son,
> Pure Wind King – three in one.
>
> – THE FOURTH LITURGICAL SUTRA: THE SUPREME[14]

The longing to address the Holy One in poetic form spans a rich diversity of Christian cultural and historical contexts, including first-century Palestine, sixth-century Ireland, and eighth-century China. Centuries later, Protestant reformer John Calvin (1509–1564) saw that the genius of the Psalms was to "portray a variety of religious moods, and this, as well as the relative shortness of each psalm, makes them adaptable for liturgical purposes..."[15]

## ENDNOTES

[1] Marcus J. Borg, *Reading the Bible Again for the First Time* (New York: HarperCollins, 2001), 143 (note 39), 146.

[2] James H. Charlesworth, ed. *The Old Testament Pseudepigrapha,* Vol. 2 (New York: Doubleday & Co. 1983), pp. 654, 748.

[3] James L. Kugel, *The Idea of Biblical Poetry* (New Haven: Yale University Press, 1981), 97.

[4] Nolan B. Harmon, *The Interpreter's Bible,* Vol. IV (Nashville: Abingdon Press, 1955), 15.

[5] Ibid., 15.

[6] Kugel, *Biblical Poetry,* 182.

[7] Ibid., 181.

[8] Ibid., 203.

[9] Ibid., 183, 187.

[10] A. F. Kirkpatrick, *The Book of Psalms* (Cambridge: Cambridge University Press, 1902), 838–40.

[11] Kugel, *Biblical Poetry,* 8.

[12] P. Murray, ed. *The Deer's Cry: A Treasury of Irish Religious Verse* (Dublin: Four Courts Press, 1986), 15.

[13] Martin Palmer, *The Jesus Sutras: Rediscovering the Lost Scrolls of Taoist Christianity* (New York: The Ballantine Publishing Group, 2001), 184–185. In 489 CE, the Roman Emperor Zeno closed the great theological college, the School of the Persians – a result of a theological dispute. It was located on the edge of the Roman Empire in the city of Edessa, northeast of the Euphrates River. The seminarians and theological scholars from that school

continued to provide leadership to a loose confederation of churches that continued to thrive east of the Roman empire within the Sassanian Empire. Over the next centuries, the Church of the East had missions and congregations in what is now present day Armenia, Azerbaijan, Iran, Iraq, Pakistan, Afghanistan, Tibet, and India. The description of this church's mission, led by Bishop Aluoben, to the Tang Dynasty in northwestern China in 635 CE, and of the Taoist Christian scriptures is found on pages 135–232 of Palmer's book.

[14] Ibid., 202–203.

[15] Harmon, *Interpreter's Bible,* 16.

# The Psalms and Other Religious Traditions

The Hebrew Psalms represent a cornerstone of the Bible and comprise a major part of the literature of both the Jewish and Christian faiths. When we begin to explore the literature and culture of other religions, we often find values, traditions, and ways of thinking and worshipping that are similar to our own. For this reason, Jews and Christians may delight in the discovery that other religions, including Islam, Hinduism, and Buddhism, have at their core a literary tradition similar to that of the Psalms. And sometimes, they are familiar with the actual Psalms themselves.

## ISLAM

Muslims, for example, know the Psalms. "The Qur'an refers repeatedly to the 'Torah,' the 'Evangel,' and the 'Psalms,' and asks Jews and Christians to abide by what they find in them."[1] At the same time, Muslim devotional literature contains many similarities to the Hebrew Psalms. *Amin* is a Muslim utterance used by whole congregations, just as *Amen* is used in Jewish and Christian liturgies.[2] The Arabic word *tasliya*, like the Hebrew *Hosanna*, is used as an acclamation in praise prayers much like the praise psalms.[3] Many themes within Islamic devotional literature address themes found in the Psalms, including sin, confession, praise, forgiveness, repentance, blessing, and calling on God's name. Often, the writers name Allah as Rock, Fortress, and Stronghold, just as the psalmists do.[4]

*Al-Sahifat Al-Sajjadiyya* is the oldest Islamic prayer manual. This Shi'a Arabic breviary is used today in Iraq, Syria, and other Islamic countries, and contains over 600 pages of devotions. Written by the great-grandson of the Prophet *'Ali Zain al-Abidin,* it is a seminal work of the early period of Islamic spirituality. Shi'ite tradition regards the *Sahifa* as worthy of veneration and ranks it behind only the Qur'an and 'Ali's *Nahj al-balagha.* The title *Al-Sahifat Al-Sajjadiyya* means "The Book of al-Sajjad." Al-Sajjad is one of the titles given to Zayn al-Abidin meaning "the one who constantly prostrates himself in prayer." The *Sahifa* has been called the "Sister of the Qur'an."

In her study of Islamic prayer manuals, *Muslim Devotions,* Constance Padwick sites psalm-like praises found in the *Al-Sahifat Al-Sajjadiyya.* Here is one *du'a,* or prayer, for the 23rd day of Ramadan:

> Thou who hast spread the earth as a plain:
> Thou who hast set the mountains as stakes:
> Thou who hast set the sun as a lamp:
> Thou who hast set the moon as a light:
> Thou who hast appointed the night as a covering:
> Thou who hast appointed the day for livelihood...[5]

Many of the verses of this holy book use parallelism and are sometimes called the "Psalms of the Household of Muhammad." The Hebrew Psalms and the "Psalms of the Household of Muhammad" also share many thoughts. For example, both Psalm 139 and the *du'a* for the 20th day of Ramadan say that one can never truly hide from God:

> I cannot seek shelter from Thee in night or day,
> on land or sea, in any hole of earth or heaven, plain or mountain;
> for neither does the overspreading night, nor the heaven with its zodiac,
> nor the sea with its waves, nor the earth with its ravines,
> nor the mountains with their eminences hide aught from Thee.[6]

A giant in the tradition of Persian mystical literature is the Qur'an commentator known as the Pir of Herat. Born Kwaja Abdullah Ansari (1006–1089 CE), he is known first and foremost for his *Munajat,* or intimate conversations with God. This collection has long served as a devotional handbook within the Muslim and Sufi traditions.[7] The style of writing in the *Munajat* overlaps the Hebrew Psalms in several significant ways. The language is intensely intimate. God is addressed personally. A whole range of emotions is brought before the Holy, including love, longing, frustration, anguish, despair, joy, and peace. Translator Wheeler M. Thackston comments that what we find in the *Munajat* is "couched in sometimes humble, sometimes reproachful language, the speaker assumes the familiar position vis-a vis God that a faithful servant of long tenure might assume in speaking to his master."[8]

The *Munajat* includes both the original sayings of Ansari and those of later poets who ascribed their writings to him. As the *Munajat* is not canonized "it is probably safe to say that no two printed versions...agree with regard to the material included."[9] Like the Hebrew Psalms, the *Munajat* relies on language that is simple, brief, and concise. The *Munajat* also features the use of parallelism. Thackston notes, "extensive use is made of the rhetorical device known as *tarsi,* where the sequence of vowels in two or more parallel lines is exactly the same, with only the consonants varying."[10] Unfortunately, certain forms of the original expression are lost in translation from Persian to English. For example, English translations are usually not able to reflect the use of the script-pun in the original. This is where two words or compounds are spelled alike in Persian but are distinct because of the introduction of an extra unwritten vowel, "as *taj-dar* ("crowned") and *taj-i-dar* ("crown of the gallows") ... the use of near homonyms such as *taát* ("obedience") and *taqat* ("endurance"), and of pseudo-etymology, where two words appear to be derived from the same root but are actually not, as *hajat* ("need") and *hujjat* ("proof, defense")..."[11]

The *Munajat* differs from the Hebrew Psalms in that it is a monologue from the servant of God *to* God. What we hear are the confessions, observations, complaints, aspirations, and laments of the servant. Unlike the Psalms, there is no attempt to give words to God in reply to the statements made by the servant.

O God,
I am annoyed by those acts of obedience
that cause me to be proud:
Happy that disobedience
that brings me to my knees.
O God,
I am helpless and perplexed.
Neither have I what I know
nor know what I have.
O God,
There is no necessity for me to fly for refuge:
Before me lies danger, with no way back.
Take my hand: I have no asylum but you.[12]

Reading this passage, the intimacy of the use of first person places us in the position of the poet. As we speak or read we are invited to identify the places within us that know the poet's meaning.

The Sufi sage Shaykh Ibn 'Ata' illah was born in Alexandria, Egypt, around 1250 CE. His writings include the *Kitah al-Hikam* (The Book of Aphorisms), a book of wisdom, and are read by many Muslims, both within and outside the Sufi tradition.[13] He has been compared to his Christian contemporary Meister Eckhart of Germany (d. ca. 1327).[14] The *Hikam* is divided into three parts: the aphorisms, treatises, and intimate discourses. Of the three, the intimate discourses most resemble the Hebrew Psalms in their personal and familiar approach to God. Here is a sample.

My God,
how near You are to me,
and how far I am from You!
My God,
how kind You are to me!
So what is it that veils me from You?
My God...
I know that it is Your desire

to make Yourself known to me in everything
so that I will not ignore You in anything.[15]

While these are not strictly psalms, they follow a pattern of parallelism. As with Kwaja Abdullah Ansari's writing, script-puns and other plays on words are woven into his verse.

## Buddhism

God acts within every moment
and creates the world within each breath.
He speaks from the center of the universe,
in the silence beyond all thought.[16]

– Stephen Mitchell, Psalm 93

A number of Buddhists have translated the Psalms to enrich their practice of meditation. Norman Fischer, co-abbot of the San Francisco Zen Center, explores the inspiration that led him to write a new translation of the Psalms from a Zen Buddhist perspective. In Zen practice, the crowd of thoughts and emotions that are catalysts to suffering need to be addressed. Contemplating a psalm can awaken one to unresolved challenges for being present. In life it is possible to avoid or evade certain experiences, people, and circumstances. A person could be part of a religious community that doesn't allow anger or conflict. Yet each person needs to come to terms with anger and conflict. From a Zen perspective, Fischer writes, the Psalms help us access "our emotional life, bringing it into consciousness and massaging it… The daily recitation evokes many emotions and gives…an ancient voice to what we feel deeply inside but might not notice… So this is what the psalms are – the daily speaking out of our deepest human longing."[17]

Fischer considers his approach to the Psalms to be "Zen-inspired." He has not translated them, but has created new versions of them, with the intention of learning from the Psalms "to expand my own understanding under their influence."[18]

For example, Psalm 22:19 reads,

But do not remain so far away, O Lord;
O my help, hasten to my aid.

– (NEB)

Fischer gives new expression to this text:

So, now, in this very place, I call on you
There is no one left

Do not be far from me
Be the center
Of the center
Of the circle
Be the strength of that center
the power of the absence that is the center...[19]

Buddhists are taught to develop a daily experience of *presence.* Focusing on breathing and awareness of one's body is a common way this is done. Born into Judaism, Fischer suggests yet another way – using a word or phrase from the Hebrew Psalms to develop this sense of presence. He suggests adopting a stance of curiosity toward whatever word or phrase you choose, perhaps asking, "What does it really mean?" He explains that "when you use a word or phrase like that it stays for a while as a word or phrase, but then after a while it dissolves as that and just becomes a feeling in the body and the heart. You could practice...just grabbing some word or phrase when it spontaneously comes up."[20]

The Hebrew understanding that suffering is part of life and must be acknowledged can balance the stance of detachment in Buddhism. Buddhism's starting place is the presence of suffering. The practice of meditation can help one gain enlightenment, the path to suffering's end. Fischer states, "The Psalms make it clear that suffering is not to be escaped or bypassed...and through that very suffering and admission of suffering, the letting go into suffering and the calling out from it, mercy and peace can come."[21]

Stephen Mitchell is another Zen-Buddhist who has given attention to the Psalms. His beautiful translations use new language to awaken a new audience of people of diverse faiths in unexpected ways.

Notice the contrast between the translation of Psalm 1:1–2 found in the New English Bible, and Mitchell's own translation:

> Happy is the man
> who does not take the wicked for his guide,
> nor walk the road that sinners tread,
> nor take his seat among the scornful,
> the law of the Lord is his delight,
> the law his meditation night and day.
>
> – (NEB)


> Blessed are the man and woman
> who have grown beyond their greed,
> and have put an end to hatred,
> and no longer nourish illusions,
> but they delight in the way things are,
> and keep their hearts open day and night.[22]
>
> – STEPHEN MITCHELL

Mitchell's choice of words allows the reader to entertain new thoughts. It is important to allow for curiosity. If we simply compare the original translation with the new version to discover which is "best," we miss the point. Each expresses a different possibility for the seeker to meditate upon. Even the contrast between the two can awaken in us new images and new meanings.

## HINDUISM

Sacred Hindu writings also contain some of the poetic devices encountered in the Psalms. In the Rgveda, we encounter a speech by the goddess Vak in the *Devi-sukta*. The Hebrew God and the Hindu deity are similar in their relationship to the natural world. In the first stanza we encounter the claims made by the goddess:

> ...I extend over all existing creatures,
> and even touch the heaven with my forehead.

I breathe a strong breath like the wind and tempest,
while I hold together all existence.
Beyond this wide earth and beyond the heavens
I have become so mighty in my grandeur.[23]

In Psalm 104, the psalmist describes the activity of God with attributes that would be familiar to a Hindu devotee:

How immensely great you are,
robed in majesty and honor,
clothed in a mantle of light.
Only you stretch out the curtain of the sky,
lay the beams of your palace in
the oceans,
make the clouds your chariot,
ride on the wings of the wind.
You make the winds your messengers,
fire and flame your servants.

— PSALM 104:1B–5A

Reading the devotional literature of a spiritual tradition different from one's own requires respect. It requires hospitality toward our neighbor, who may be friend or stranger. It also invites spiritual seekers to root themselves in their own tradition while cultivating the spiritual values of respect, love, and wisdom.

## ENDNOTES

1 Tarif Khalidi, *The Muslim Jesus: Sayings and Stories in Islamic Literature* (Cambridge: Harvard University Press, 2001), 19.
2 Constance E. Padwick, *Muslim Devotions* (Oxford, England: Oneworld Publications, 1996), 108.
3 Ibid., 166.
4 Ibid., 25.
5 Ibid., 250.
6 Ibid., 251.

[7] Victor Danner and Wheeler M. Thackston, *Ibn 'Ata' Illah: The Book of Wisdom; Kwaja Abdullah Ansari: Intimate Conversations* (New York: Paulist Press, 1978), 165.

[8] Ibid., 175.

[9] Ibid., 178.

[10] Ibid., 176.

[11] Ibid., 177.

[12] Ibid., 189, 191, 211.

[13] Ibid., 3.

[14] Ibid., 16.

[15] Ibid., 121.

[16] Stephen Mitchell, *A Book of Psalms: Selected & Adapted from the Hebrew* (New York: HarperCollins, 1993), 42.

[17] Meg Funk, "Norman Fischer's New Translation of the Psalms," *Monastic Inter-religious Dialogue,* Bulletin 69, August 2002, Washington, DC.

[18] Norman Fischer, *Opening to You: Zen-Inspired Translations of the Psalms* (New York: Viking, 2002), xiii.

[19] Ibid., 32–33.

[20] Funk, "Norman Fischer's New Translation of the Psalms."

[21] Fischer, *Opening to You,* xvi.

[22] Stephen Mitchell, *A Book of Psalms: Selected & Adapted from the Hebrew* (New York: HarperCollins, 1993), 3.

[23] Klaus K. Klostermaier, *Hindu Writings: A Short Introduction to Major Sources* (Oxford, England: Oneworld Publications, 2000), 85.

# Notes on Pre-Columbian Literature and the Psalm to Quetzalcoatl

Mexican literature dates back to more than 2,000 years BCE, the period when scholars believe the Mayas invented paper books. The Spanish Inquisition burnt most of those books, but petroglyphs and the oral tradition fortunately survived. Moreover, many codices were reconstructed from memory by priests.

Nezahualcoyotl (1402–1471), a warring Aztec king turned pacifist, was Mexico's foremost Nahuatl-language exponent of "song and flower," as poetry was referred to. He sang to the fleetingness of life and beauty. Sor Juana Ines de la Cruz (1648–1695), a scholarly nun, was known for her enthralling love poetry. Octavio Paz (1914–1998) drew from his predecessors to write the mystical-erotic poetry that won him the Nobel Prize in 1990.

Mexican mythology is as complex and as irreducible as the mythologies of India, Egypt, and Greece. According to the Aztecs – a term which here subsumes all other pre-Columbian cultures in Mexico – the vertical dimension of the cosmos had several tiers of heavens, and levels of the underworld; very much like a skyscraper with underground parking lots. The highest or 13th level was the "place of duality," or the "place of the creator of all." Below that were many deities representing different aspects of life on earth, very much like saints in the Catholic Church representing different virtues.

And then there was Quetzalcoatl, the Plumed Serpent. He was a deity who fell from ideal purity to a state of human weakness. He is said to have gone into exile by fashioning a raft of serpents and setting off across the seas. But he vowed to return, and this is how he played an unwitting role in the fall of the mighty Aztec empire. When the Aztecs sighted bearded Spaniards disembarking from their ships, they thought Quetzalcoatl had returned and hence initially offered little or no resistance. Of course, the pox brought from Europe, horses, and superior military technology contributed to the conquest of Mexico.

My Psalm to Quetzalcoatl (on page 163) is a humble but sincere nod to the rich cultural tradition of my native land.

— © Maya Khankhoje.

# Index of Scripture and Other Sacred Writing

**A**

Akkadian
Curse of Agade **196**
Aztec
Huitzilopochtli **18**
Madrid Codex **46**

**C**

Canaanite **198**

**D**

Dead Sea Scrolls
Book of Hymns **22**
Book of Hymns 2:3–5 **22**
Deuteronomy 23:7 **117**
Deuteronomy 30:15, 19–20 **111**

**E**

Egyptian
Hymn to Aten **194**
Hymn to the Sun God **82**
English
Lavender Blue – Old Nursery
Rhyme **24**
Exodus 3:7–8 **133**

**H**

Hindu **46**
Poem by Tulsidas **46**
Rgveda, Devi-sukta **217**

**I**

Irish
The Questions of Ethne Alba **20**
Book of Invasions – Amergin **207**

**L**

Lamentations 4:5 **21**
Lao-tzu **38**
Leviticus 19:17–18 **116**

Leviticus 19:18b **116**
Luke 1:46–55 **206**
Luke 2:29–32 **206**

**M**

2 Maccabees 2:13 **191**
Muslim
Du'a
for 20th day of Ramadan **212**
for 23rd day of Ramadan **212**
for 27th day of Ramadan **45**
Kitah al-Hikam **214**
The Munajat **214**
Ganjul Arsh **16**

**P**

Proverbs 17:28 **82**
Psalm 1:1–2 **217**
Psalm 1:1–6 **83**
Psalm 5:1–3a **13**
Psalm 6:6 **31**
Psalm 18:1 **31**
Psalm 20:7 **122**
Psalm 21:8–10 **115**
Psalm 21 (revised) **118**
Psalm 22:19 **215**
Psalm 23:4 **31**
Psalm 33 **45**
Psalm 35:10 **19**
Psalm 37:1–3 **84**
Psalm 37:16 **23**
Psalm 41:4–5 **18**
Psalm 42:9 **19**
Psalm 46:1–5 **128**
Psalm 49:16–17 **21**
Psalm 51:1–4, 10–13 **71–72**
Psalm 52:8 **30**
Psalm 55:2–5 **32**
Psalm 63:1, 11 **85**
Psalm 68:1–2 **96**

Psalm 72:1–3, 12–14a **122**
Psalm 74:1 **20**
Psalm 74:4–9 **196**
Psalm 77:1 **25**
Psalm 77:33, 56, 72 **98**
Psalm 78:2–10 **60–61**
Psalm 83:13–15 **16**
Psalm 84:2 **32**
Psalm 85:10 **9**
Psalm 91:1-4a, 5, 11 **79**
Psalm 92:9 **198**
Psalm 93:3 **25**
Psalm 93:25 **215**
Psalm 98 **133**
Psalm 101:1–3 **207**
Psalm 101:1–6a **109**
Psalm 104:19–20, 22–23 **47**
Psalm 104:1b–5a **218**
Psalm 104:2b–3a **47**
Psalm 104:32 **47**
Psalm 107:29 **27**
Psalm 108:1–7 **108**
Psalm 108:12–13 **108**
Psalm 109:23–24 **27**
Psalm 116:1–2 **27**
Psalm 118:1–4 **26**
Psalm 137:9 **118**
Psalm 138:1–8 **55**

Psalm 145:13 **198**
Psalm 148:1 **17**
Psalm 148:1–5, 8–10 **57**
*Pseudepigrapha*
    Odes to Solomon 15 **204**
    Psalms of Solomon 3:1–2 **203**

**R**
Rumi
    *My Worst Habit* **19**
    *The Guest House* **119**

**S**
Sanskrit
    Salutation of the Dawn **81**
Stafford, William
    *The Way It Is* **13**
    *A Ritual to Read to One Another* **119**
Song of Songs 1:12 **24**
Song of Songs 5:3 **21**
Sumerian
    *Enuma Elish* **193**

**T**
Taoist Christian
    Fourth Liturgical Sutra **208**
    Second Liturgical Sutra **208**

RAY MCGINNIS is available to offer workshops tailored for writers' groups, academic groups including secondary schools, congregations, synagogues and mosques, bookstores and libraries, community centres, healthcare facilities, retreat settings, and professional groups. He has taught writing workshops to over 3,500 participants in various settings since 1999.

You can contact Ray McGinnis by:
E-MAIL:   raymundo@writetotheheart.com
PHONE:   604-408-4457
ADDRESS:  2095 Beach Avenue, #403,
          Vancouver, BC V6G 1Z3

AUTHOR PHOTO BY: MATTHEW JACOBS PHOTOGRAPHY, VANCOUVER, BC